INTERNARRA

Placing the Self

SECOND EDITION

Ajit K. Maan

University Press of America,® Inc.
Lanham · Boulder · New York · Toronto · Plymouth, UK

Copyright © 2010 by
University Press of America,® Inc.
4501 Forbes Boulevard
Suite 200
Lanham, Maryland 20706
UPA Acquisitions Department (301) 459-3366

Estover Road
Plymouth PL6 7PY
United Kingdom

Library of Congress Control Number: 2009938609
ISBN: 978-0-7618-4967-4 (paperback : alk. paper)
eISBN: 978-0-7618-4968-1

For:

Sohni and Simrin

Contents

Foreword

As someone regularly thinking about the professional practice of counseling and mediation, I am always interested in concepts that enable effective and ethically justifiable forms of practice. The question that continually demands attention is, "What concepts produce the most value or leverage when they are applied in practice?" Those who theorize professional practice are always debating the comparative value of the many different approaches to the work of the helping professions. In these fields models of practice of different degrees of elaboration abound. There are those who argue that the differences between such theories and models should be interrogated in relation to empirical data with regard to their effectiveness. There is no doubt value in this kind of evaluation but often the empirical endeavor does not quite produce conclusive accounts of the value of particular conceptualizations of practice.

Ajit Maan's book represents another approach to the determination of value for concepts that might be drawn upon to guide practice. It is the philosopher's approach of interrogating the meaning of concepts. The promise of this approach lies in the testing of the robustness of meanings or concepts through systematic thought. If concepts are to serve as the useful building blocks of practice then it is necessary that they should have a certain material strength and a certain flexibility of use. If they do not stand up to such tests then they should be jettisoned and reshaped just as surely as if they failed the empirical tests of effectiveness.

Because I have a commitment to the forms of practice that have evolved under the headings of narrative therapy and narrative mediation, I am particularly interested in the concepts of narrative and of identity that Ajit Maan works over in this book. Therapy in my definition is about the construction of a working narrative of identity that enables a person to live life in a preferred direction. And conflict resolution practice is about something similar for a relationship. Mediation, for example, involves two or more people working to construct a narrative of relationship that enables them to perform concerted action, or joint action (as John Shotter, 1994, calls it). I am interested in exploring the leverage that can be gained from thinking of people's struggles to live meaningful lives in narrative terms. Thinking of people as meaning making beings and thinking of narrative forms as basic to meaning making activity holds, to my ear, much greater promise than thinking of persons as collections of stimulus-response bonds or as reducible to biological inner drives. It has already been shown to generate a degree of decidability about life for many people. I believe it is the most promising alternative to the more essentialist options that have been taken up by others in the therapeutic and conflict resolution domains.

I am therefore grateful for the chance to engage with the work Ajit Maan does in this book. It constitutes the spadework that turns over the soil of a conceptual field and aerates it with clear thinking. Her work allows me and others to plant seedlings of practice that use these concepts and to nurture their growth. So what exactly is the work that Ajit Maan has done and what promise does it hold?

The central task that Ajit Maan sets herself is to interrogate some rigid notions of narrative and identity that she identifies in the work of Paul Ricoeur. Her aim is to pry open some tightly bound concepts in Ricoeur's theorizing in order to make room for greater flexibility in the construction of identity narratives. In particular, she disputes Ricoeur's reliance on Aristotle's "concordance," or narrative unity. Ricoeur's conception of a narrative is not "polyphonic," she points out. But she goes further than calling for alternative narratives. She also calls for alternative narrative *structures*. Without rethinking the structure of a satisfying narrative to accommodate multiple narrative forms, there is always the possibility of a subordinate narrative identity being actively repressed by the simple requirement of narrative unity.

This point is a critical one for narrative practice. One of the central departures of narrative practice from other approaches to therapy has focused on this very point. Too often the requirement for narrative unity in the therapeutic world has privileged the expertise of the therapist over the local knowledge of the client. Too often narratives of diagnostic categorization have totalized the identities of persons whose identity stories might be appreciated in quite different terms through an alternative understanding of identity. Too often in mediation the assumption that all conflicts arise out of individual interests has sidelined other stories of relational cooperation. Too often the singular narratives of family drawn from patriarchal, middle class, European traditions have structured conversations in both therapy and family mediation to exclude the alternative identity narrative. Narrative practice has been at pains to open up new bases for the construction of identity narratives in these domains.

There have, however, been many worried responses to these efforts that have voiced a concern about the loss of narrative unity in favor of some kind of relativistic, formless multiplicity that gives no grounds for identity coherence at all. Ajit Maan provides us with a response that addresses this concern as well. She outlines a theory of narrative structure that allows for the possibility of coherence rather than fragmentation while including competing narratives as sources for identity construction. She calls the resulting identity projects "internarrative identities" because they contain nuances drawn from subordinated narratives and alongside elements of master narratives that are not able to be ignored.

It is perhaps no coincidence that Ajit Maan is able to draw upon her own Indian cultural background, on women's narratives, and on the writing of an Indian novelist, Meena Alexander, to sketch out the possibility of a multiplicity of narratives giving shape to a life. In the aftermath of the critique of patriarchy, and of the "grand" era of European colonization (although this does not mean that patriarchy has withered in the face of critique, or that all colonizing is over, or that new forms of colonizing practice are not still occurring) we are all living in the midst a kind of tension between the master narratives of the colonizer and the de-colonizing impulse that produces a transcendent hope for greater freedom and moral agency. That this tension is most acutely sensed by those who are assigned the subaltern position in the colonizing narrative, or in the patriarchal narrative of the family, is perhaps not surprising. It is nevertheless a feature of the condition in which we all live in the late modern world, whether we are positioned in the subaltern position or in a position of at least some degree of privilege. Ajit Maan's argument is that we actually live with narrative complexity and must necessarily do the work of identity production out of the stuff of competing narratives.

For those subaltern voices to whom Ajit Maan's ear is attuned, the Western tradition of narrative unity "requires too much experiential negation." It is to the opposite trajectory of experiential affirmation that she turns to find plot elements that deserve to be included in a more nuanced account of internarrative identity. These plot elements are grounded in the spaces people occupy in their lives. They are stored in memory, not just cognitively, but also kinesthetically. They are plot elements that do not fit within dominant cultural narratives and they deserve to be included in the identity accounts that people develop. Ajit Maan conjures up Roy Schafer (among others) to answer Ricoeur's reliance on narrative unity and to assert that narrative multiplicity is less problematic than narrative unity. For Schafer, the reduction of narratives to a singular representation of a self involves the diminishment of a person. It requires an unhealthy repression.

To my ear, these ideas are refreshing. There has been too much emphasis in psychology on concepts like congruence and wholeness and the integration of experience into a singular self. Why not celebrate narrative multiplicity and concentrate on the elaboration of identity narratives that draw upon more than one narrative source? Why not allow for contradiction and inconsistency of representation and value the extra resources that might be drawn upon as a result? Why not plug for some form of internarrative identity? As Michael White said, "I have not met many people who live a single-storied life" (Winslade & Hedtke, 2008).

When people experience the distress that comes with the diminishment of their identity stories in the face of dominant master narratives, they turn sometimes to professionals for help. What they do not need at such moments is to be forced back into narrative unity. For practitioners of narrative therapy and narrative mediation, what Ajit Maan has written can be taken as encouragement and justification. It offers philosophical validation and robust articulation of a perspective that is often implicitly understood by those who work with people.

But Ajit Maan offers more specific assistance than just general encouragement. She points to a number of places where elements of internarrative identity might be sought out. She also stresses the importance of working for narrative coherence (without singularity). In these ways she sets those of us interested in narrative practice a task. It is the task of working more assiduously and intentionally at the process of narrative construction in conversation. Her work deserves to be mined for its detailed suggestions.

One such detail is her distinction between the narratives that govern public and private selves. She suggests that private narratives often contain invigorating narrative elements that must be suppressed in the face of public power and that the answer need not always involve the making public of what is private and precious. Her internarrative identity is about the integration of internarrative associations (drawn from memory and from embodiment) without a requirement for a unified representation. The work of creating these internarrative associations (or crossovers) is always fluid, forever ongoing, and never complete. It is also an exercise of agency.

While Ajit Maan draws many of her examples from literature it is easy to imagine the processes of narrative construction she refers to taking place in conversation. If therapeutic conversation can be considered a genre of conversation dedicated to the construction of identity narratives, then these concepts are rich with possibility. I look forward to using them as a prism for the ongoing refraction of light in my own work. (John Winslade, Los Angeles, 2009)

References

Shotter, J. *Conversational realities: Constructing life through language.* Thousand Oaks, CA: Sage. 1994.

Winslade, J. and L. Hedtke. Michael White: Fragments of an event. *The International Journal for Narrative Therapy and Community Work, 2008* (2), 2008. 73-79.

Preface

Narrative conflict, the conflict of competing "truths" of one's life, is a familiar problem for most of us. How does one describe one's life in a way that is unified and complete when there are competing versions of the events of a life? What if one no longer associates oneself with one's past actions? How can one's autobiography encompass all that one is when there is a feeling of having lived many lives, in various places, with many beginnings and multiple endings? The challenge is even more daunting for those who experience the conflict of cultures, languages, and conceptual systems, in the telling of their life-stories.

This work locates the solution to the problem within the problem itself. The argument is that existence *in-between* authoritarian discourses of dominant cultures, enables an extended form of agency wherein a subject is able to undermine traditional associations, assumptions, and concepts, and at the same time, create links between otherwise incommensurable world views.

The normative ideal of narrative unity and resulting unified self-silence not only other narrative forms but other voices, other selves, other ways of being. We make ourselves who we are by making our experiences meaningful. Events and experiences do not have meaning in themselves; meaning is determined by association and a narrator can extend her agency by extending her field of association. But the type of associations one can make are restricted by the requirements of narrative unity. Traditionally in the West, the meaning of an even or experience is determined by its temporal orientation in a linear plot. Internarrative Identity is based upon re-association. Internarrative associations involve *space* and *place* rather than strictly temporal association.

Not only is the traditional Western quest for narrative unity misguided, those subjects who have been marginalized by the concept of a single unified subjectivity are actually in a privileged position for cultural critique, and more importantly, for extended narrative agency. Rather than being a passive recipient of dominant discourses, the Internarrative Subject is uniquely able to subvert regulatory identity practices and create alternative linkings and associations.

Acknowledgments

The author expresses sincere appreciation to Nancy Tuana and Mark Johnson for their guidance and persistent enthusiasm for this project and to Steven Shakman and Cheyney Ryan for their assistance in the preparation of this manuscript.

The author gratefully acknowledges permission to quote from *Fault Lines: A Memoir* by Meena Alexander (The Feminist Press at the City University of New York, 2003). Copyright 1993 by Meena Alexander. Reprinted by permission of the author and the Feminist Press at the City University of New York.

Introduction

While contemporary inquiries into the nature of the "self" are inclined to allow previously marginalized groups to assert their status as subjects, and their stories as narratives, the postmodern denial of authorship and deconstruction of the self as a linguistic construction throws this entire inquiry into question. Roland Barthes[1] has proclaimed "The Death of the Author" arguing that the first-person "I" is nothing more than "an instance of saying I" and the author is nothing more than an instance of writing. And Foucault undermines the identification of the author with the text, by asking, "What matter who is speaking?"[2] But for some of us, the question of who is speaking is of crucial importance. While deconstruction calls autobiography into question by problematizing the authority and source of any utterance, others point out that postmodern deconstruction of subjectivity is a luxury of the privileged. As Rosi Braidotti puts it, "in order to announce the death of the subject one must have gained the right to speak as one."[3]

Paul Ricoeur sees himself as providing a solution to the recent debates concerning the status of the subject. His solution is to distinguish two senses of "identity:" "*idem*" from "*ipse*." Contemporary theories of subjectivity, Ricoeur argues, consider identity in only one of its forms—*idem*—or identity as distinguishing characteristics which remain the same over time. This is the form assumed by the liberal notion of personal identity which has been deconstructed by the postmodern practitioner. But what postmodern critique has overlooked, according to Ricoeur, is another sense of identity. This is a sense of identity which is developed as a result of the narrative mediation between *idem*-identity assumed by the modernist, and *ipse* or self-identity. (*Ipse* is the type of intentional self-consistency exemplified by the act of keeping a promise in spite of changes in values or circumstances). The third type of identity created in the process of mediating *ipse* and *idem* is Narrative Identity. The narrative mediation between *idem* and *ipse* is Ricoeur's answer to the postmodern assault on the subject. This type of identity has an ethical dimension. It is a product of will and intention as much as it is a product of culture, and it is relatively stable.

Ricoeur's narrative strategy works to solve St. Augustine's problem with the discordance of experienced time, by imposing an Aristotelian *muthos* to synthesize discordant experience. Poetic emplotment becomes the imaginative technique whereby an otherwise fractured and fluctuating subject constitutes herself. The authorial desire of the self-constituting subject affects the way in which the involuntary conditions of the plot are understood. Narrating is the transformative element. So even when a subject cannot alter the involuntary aspects of her situation, she can re-figure the way she understands them. One can provide the involuntary with alternative meanings.

I agree with Ricoeur that focusing exclusively on a self-as-same subject model seems misguided, but I will argue that the exclusive focus on Aristotelian plot structure in the West has caused a marginalization of narratives based on other constructions of experience. Rather than assimilating difference into a unitary concept of identity, we should allow theoretical room for what Ricoeur calls the "insurmountable fissures" of experience *and* the connections made and re-made. Narrative Identity theorists are convinced that if we don't structure our lives/stories/experiences in the traditional form, we will not be able to reflect upon and give meaning to the bulk of our experiences taken together. That is to say that narrative is a method whereby the experiences of a life time can be provided with meaning by tying them together in a certain "culturally sanctioned"[4] structure.

But it seems to me that as a narrator I have more than two choices. The first choice is the classical one in which the meaning assigned to experiences and events depends on their place in the meta-narrative. The second choice is the one postmodernism has been held accountable for—a narrative which is a disconnected litany of experiences. But I think that we as narrators can view our lives retrospectively and narrate in a way that takes all or most of our experiences into account in any particular telling of any part of the story. We can consider the entire story in the telling of any particular part of the story. We can see connections between causes and effects, and repeating patterns, without narrating a story with formal unity. I will argue that narrative unity and wholeness are not required in order to have a coherent personal identity.

Aristotelian *muthos,* or emplotment, is a process of making the intelligible out of the accidental, the universal from the singular, the necessary from the episodic.[5] But there are different kinds of narrative practice—practice that represents disjunctive and nonlinear subjectivity. This type of practice is aligned with the postmodern suspicion of identity, and yet it recognizes the imperative for situating an already marginal subject. This is a technique whereby even a subaltern subject can simultaneously assume subjectivity *and* maintain the disruptive potential that her standpoint guarantees.

While canonical Western narratives associate identity with formal integrity, it has been noted that women's narratives often seem formless and may be disconnected and fragmentary, rather than being traditionally ordered. While the canonical autobiography relates the imposition of order on the flux of existence, women's stories have embraced and represented the flux.[6] Alicia Ostriker observes that another characteristic of women's personal stories is the elimination of distance between past and present.[7] Rachel DuPlessis defines a female aesthetic as fluid, non-linear, decentralized, multi-voiced, non-hierarchic.[8] And Elaine Showalter has argued that the unique character of women's writing results from drawing on female bodily images, using a "woman's language," and reflects women's complex cultural position.[9] Nadya Aisenberg insists that texts centered around a linear quest fail to authenticate experience like hers and that "coherent stories simply do not correspond to our experience of life."[10] These types of assertions respond to an aesthetic movement represented by Walter Pater who argued that traditional masculine aesthetics are superior in form because the masculine aesthetic is defined by "the maintenance of a standard," which, "follows a spirit of construction as opposed to what is literally incoherent or ready to fall to pieces, and in opposition to what is hysteric or works at random."[11]

The precise nature of a female aesthetic, if there is one, is a matter of continuing controversy, fraught with charges of essentialism. Even so, I am interested in a central goal of feminist criticism which continues to be the deconstruction of the normative masculine formal requirements which consider women's writing incohesive and indeterminate. I will argue, in the chapters which follow, that textual discontinuity results from experienced nonlinearity and that these textual qualities are deliberate strategies to subvert authoritarian modes of self-representation.

The following chapters will identify and problematize the compositional criteria within which Narrative Identity is constructed. These criteria would exclude, on the basis of structural deviation, alternative forms of self-narration. In the traditional model, it is not just the configurational competence of the narrator which is in question, but the intelligibility, rationality, the very identity of the narrator is at stake.

I will argue that the aesthetic foundation of Paul Ricoeur's Narrative Identity Theory results in a particular conception of personal identity which is problematic. While embracing the central thesis of Narrative Identity Theory, I argue that the exclusionary aesthetic (an aesthetic which relegates a non-unified narrative to the status of non-narrative) in Ricoeur's conception of "plot" is at the root of his linking of identity with consistency over time. As a result, too much experience has to be left out of a unified plot. The experience that cannot be assimilated by the unified plot structure is silenced, suppressed, or trivialized. Experience is dichotomized as meaningful/trivial, anomaly/pattern, concordant/discordant. Narrative Identity Theory will be invigorated by a more inclusive notion of plot. I envision a form of subjectivity co-constructed as much by fissure and disjuncture as by intentional self consistency.

Because Narrative Identity is so compelling as a theory of personal identity, and because the theory is grounded in an Aristotelian *muthos* (imparted with temporal orientation), I argue that the classical conception of "plot" be expanded to include other structural forms. Doing so would produce two results.

First, subjects would have optimal narrative choice. Not only could a narrator tell a variety of stories; a narrator could tell a story in a variety of ways. I am not suggesting abandoning Aristotelian plot altogether. It should be one among many narrative styles, but I *am* critical of it because it restricts the assignment of meaning to experience, and limits retrospective re-tellings of personal narratives as well as present experience, and future actions. I think Rebecca Goldstein is right on the mark when she says, "The aesthetic preference for wholeness will often lead us to actions we would not otherwise undertake."[12] It is because I agree that plot is a central feature of Narrative Identity, that I argue that liberalizing plot structure is an essential aspect of maximizing agency. My thesis enlivens the sense in which narrative is self-constitutive. Narration becomes a method of extending agency.

Second, conceptions of personal identity would be altered with the introduction of structural forms that do not privilege unity and cohesion. In the traditional model identity ends up being made of all the experience which is assimilated by the narrative. It is all that which hangs together. The answer to the question "who am I?" turns out to be: I am the self who is at least unintentionally consistent (*idem*) and at best intentionally consistent (*ipse*). A more compelling answer to the question "who am I?" would be: I am the one that provides meaning for my experiences.

An alternative subjectivity locates the co-authorship of herself in the act, the meaning-giving act, of narration. I will ask myself what this sort of subjectivity looks like and I will locate an example in Meena Alexander's memoir, *Fault Lines*.[13] As the title indicates, Alexander narratively constructs herself around the places of rupture in her experience. This will prove to be not only an example of the extended subject of narrative identity (the subject formed in relation to the plot as described by Ricoeur but who also chooses the principles by which she structures her story) but also an example of a narrative choice which locates personal identity in precisely the last place Ricoeur would locate it.

The first chapter is two-fold. First I will describe the three major features of narrative subject construction. Then I will expose the classical aesthetic foundation of this type of identity and show how this foundation determines the structure of identity. I will demonstrate how the Narrative Identity of a subject is dependent upon the creation of structural unity.

The notion of discordant concordance is introduced as a characteristic, according to Ricoeur, of all narrative composition; it is the synthesis of heterogeneous. The art of narrative composition is to "configure" discordant experience into a concordant structure. While a state of complete concordance is never reached, it is the continuing function of the narrative subject to strive for concordance. Narration describes what were once discordant events as a necessary stage in the advancing plot. So, the primary difference between description and narrative lies in the status of events. In other words, narrative bestows meaning on what were previously discordant events. The problem with this idea is that the meaning that events are assigned will depend on the plot one is involved with and since the plot has a very specific structure, the meaning assigned to events will depend upon structural requirements.

Ricoeur is very explicit about what narrative should *not* be. First, a plot should *not* imitate reality in the sense of duplicating it. Character, thought, or action should *not* be privileged over plot structure. A narrative should *not* be polyphonic. And narrative structure must be closed-ended, whole, and unified. These criteria exclude the work of several of the founders of the English novel, and the work of Goethe,

Schiller, Dostoevski, Virginia Woolf, and, I will argue, the work of a particular type of narrator. *That* type of narrator, the narrator whose story these criteria hit the hardest, tend to be female narrators, narrators with multiple linguistic backgrounds, and narrators whose experiential discordance is not limited to the temporal but is complicated by repeated cultural upheaval.

The second chapter introduces the memoir *Fault Lines* as an example of a problematic case of identity within the Ricoeurean system. This narrator's life experience is too radically fractured to fit easily into classical structure. Those structural requirements demand more from a form of life like hers than from other forms of life because the more discontinuous one's experience is, the more difficult the configurational task. The extent to which narrative can provide experience with meaning is limited by the very thing that is required of traditional narrative—its structure. The work of Gayatri Spivak, Nita Kumar, Judith Butler, and Rosi Braidotti will provide the theoretical backdrop for Alexander's alternative practice.

The third chapter provides a comparative textual analysis of *Fault Lines* and traditional narrative structure in order to demonstrate precisely how *Fault Lines* fails to meet Ricoeur's aesthetic criteria—"unity," "completeness," "univocity," and "temporal orientation." My argument will be that Alexander has a coherent identity, not *in spite of* her structural choices, but *because* of them.

The fourth chapter asks what, *within* the traditional system, Alexander's aesthetic failure means for her personal identity. I will show how the non-adherence to structural requirements makes the narrator's identity *appear* incoherent, irrational, and unethical. Narrative Identity is not just emplotted; it is emplotted in a very specific narrative structure. I will argue that the identity of the narrator is determined as much by the structure of the narrative as by the content of the narrative. And I will argue that *Fault Lines* is a "narrative" nonetheless since it satisfies what I will argue is the only sufficient condition for narrative—holding the fragments of life together and assigning them temporary and provisional meaning in relation to one another. This assigning, or association, I argue, *is* an act of structuring. In this chapter I propose an alternative to Narrative Identity, an alternative I call "Internarrative Identity."

Then I will look beyond the example provided by *Fault Lines* to argue, in the fifth chapter, that classical aesthetic requirements, when applied to autobiography, actually require a psychological process of repression. The stories we tell, the identity we form, the way we understand events in our lives (the way we give them meaning) and our future actions, are in large part determined by a tacitly assumed aesthetic. Even narrators without Meena Alexander's experiential upheaval have trouble fitting their lives into this inherited structure, and fitting our lives into this structure requires negation, repression. The rationality of a traditional narrator lies in configurational competence; it is evidenced by proficiency in the homogenizing operation of Aristotelian *muthos*. I call this homogenizing operation, when applied to one's life experiences, repression. Then I will contextualize the claims of the preceding chapters within contemporary Ricoeur scholarship, and argue that

Ricoeur scholars who are interested in identity have overlooked the significance of the connection between the *function* of Aristotelian structure in *Time and Narrative,* and the *assumption* of that structure in identity formation in *Oneself as Another.*

My project as a whole is not simply to make an argument which legitimizes alternative narratives but rather to suggest that alternative narrative *structures* are in order. I agree with the basic ideas of Narrative Identity Theory: our actions make sense only in the context of our stories, that we re-create ourselves through the stories we tell, and that narrative is a way to give meaning to or appropriate the involuntary. But I will argue that narrative can function in these capacities without homogenizing experience.

Narrative Identity is a solution to the status of the unstable postmodern subject. The claim is that narrative is the element which holds together the fractured self and if narrative were not structured in Aristotelian form it would simply imitate, repeat, experiences of flux, and contingency. But I am suggesting that there is spacious middle ground between a mere chronology of disconnected events, and Aristotelian composition. The following is an exploration of middle ground—of what I call "Internarrative."

Chapter I

Narrative Identity

One implication of Ricoeur's philosophy of the subject, Narrative Identity Theory, is that the narration of life stories is guided by the principles of classical aesthetics. This means several things. It means that the meaning assigned to present experience, narrations of past experience, and future action, will conform to certain principles of emplotment. And, if Ricoeur is right, and I think he is, it means that personal identity will be developed in accordance with those same aesthetic principles.

In this chapter I will explore all the aspects of Narrative Identity as it is brought to completion in *Oneself as Another*,[1] Ricoeur's most recent work. In the first part of this chapter I examine, in three sections, the three major features of the hermeneutics of self. The first section will establish reflective mediation as a primary aspect of the immediate positioning of the subject. The second section analyzes Ricoeur's two senses of identity. And the third section explores the role of otherness in the constitution of the self.

In the second part of this chapter I argue that the structural criteria for "narrative" that Ricoeur outlines in *Time and Narrative* is imported into a theory of personal identity in *Oneself as Another*. To understand what Ricoeur means by "narrative" we must go back to the earlier work. The project of *Time and Narrative* was to solve St. Augustine's problem of the experiential discordance of time, with the imposition of an extension of Aristotelian *muthos*. The emphasis on unity and wholeness as it concerns personal identity in *Oneself as Another* is a result of his understanding of "narrative" in *Time and Narrative*. In this earlier work Ricoeur is very clear about what kinds of structures are included in the category "narrative" and which kinds of structures are excluded.

Narrating is at bottom a process of endowing experience with meaning, but this process is determined by tacitly assumed aesthetic principles. So, in the second part of this chapter, labeled "Narrative Criteria," I will argue that: 1) Ricoeur's conception of narrative rests on classical aesthetic principles, 2) that he both explicitly argues for this and implicitly assumes it, and 3) that Ricoeur marginalizes alternative narrative constructions.

Part I: The Hermeneutics of Self

Section 1: Reflective Mediation

Ricoeur's entire hermeneutic is led by the question "who?" Who is speaking, acting, narrating? Who is the subject? The answer to this question is located between the philosophy of language and the philosophy of action. The focus is on speech acts about action in which the speaker is also the agent of action. He asks what action teaches about its agent and how action and agency related to *idem* and *ipse*?[2] The conflation of these two senses of identity (characteristic sameness over time, and intentional commitment to remain the same over time in spite of changes in circumstance) has been responsible for contemporary discussions about the life or death of the modern subject.[3]

Ricoeur argues that the postmodern attack on modern subjectivity actually only attacks one part or aspect of selfhood. It attacks the idea of an autonomous self with a fixed nature. This is the part of self-identity which is demonstrated by characteristic sameness over time. But, Ricoeur says there is another type of identity and this second type is connected to ethical intention. This is the ethical intention to remain the same in the face of change and to "safeguard the institution of language" within which promises are made. However, it is a third type of identity that Ricoeur is interested in, Narrative Identity, which connects the previous two senses of identity. It is this third type of identity that will be the focus of this chapter, but let us work our way into the problem the way Ricoeur does.

Oneself as Another begins with a linguistic approach to the problem of identity which concentrates on reference. A self turns out to be one of those types of things which we can distinguish by means of identifying reference.[4] Ricoeur begins with the Strawsonian view that there are two types of things—physical objects and people. Physical objects are primary particulars because they have spatio-temporal location, while people are referents for two kinds of predicates—physical and psychological. The linguistic acts which individuate with reference to the speaker include: proper names, descriptions, pronouns, demonstratives, adverbs of place and time, and verb tenses. Another linguistic approach, following the lead of Austin and Searle, focuses on speech acts. The distinction between performatives and constatives is stressed; the latter designates a state of affairs while the former accomplishes the very thing stated by virtue of being stated. Performatives are particularly important. Ricoeur's example of a performative is making a promise.

One commits oneself in the very act of promising. This example will eventually play an important role in Ricoeur's account of the determination of ethical subjectivity. Ethical subjectivity will be tied to a certain type of intention (the intention to challenge the changes that occur over time) which is articulated with conviction.

Ricoeur insists that the problem with analytic philosophy of action is that it focuses exclusively on connecting *what* will count as an action with *Why* an action is taken, in order to distinguish between an event and an action.[5] An event simply happens and actions are what makes things happen. But this connection is made at the expense of the notion of agency. Let me clarify. Ricoeur is critical of the way "intention" is treated by analytic philosophy of action. Focusing only on reasons and causes leaves out the agent who acts. This is a conceptual linking of action and motive on one side and event and cause on the other. There is a difference between the "language games" of action and event, and one of the implications of this difference is that motives become conceptually distinct from causes. As Ricoeur puts it, "our motives for acting can in no way be assimilated to the causes by which we explain natural events."[6]

In psychoanalysis, an area of study which challenges the separation of action and movement and motive and cause, Ricoeur finds an exception to the conceptual split between action and event.[7] Psychoanalytic explanation brings into view motives that are causes.[8] For example, unconscious feelings are causally relevant. And analytic philosophy of action marginalizes the particular sense of "intention" as "presently intending to do something in the future." Ricoeur blames the Davidsonian ontology of events and the Strawsonian ontology of things in general for the lack of enduring analysis of the relations between action and agent in contemporary action theory, "In my opinion, it is the exclusive concern with the truth of the description that tends to overshadow any interest in assigning the action to its agent. Assigning the action to an agent poses a problem of veracity and no longer a problem of truth."[9] The problem is that the "truth" of an intention claim depends upon the non-verifiable statement of the agent. For example, my promise to keep a friends' secret is an attestation, an avowal, as to my intent. But the kind of truth-claim one can make about an intention is different than a truth-claim one can make about, say, a description of an event. We don't speak in terms of my intention being "true" but it may be regarded as sincere or insincere. What is needed then is a theory of ethical subjectivity that can accommodate "intending to in the future." It is here that attestation comes in.

Attestation concerns certainty—certainty appropriate to reflection and analysis. Attestation is testimony that has a type of credence which invokes trust rather than suspicion. The example is again making a promise. The performative act of making a promise is attestation. It is a "veritative" mode; it is fundamentally "attestation of the self."[10] It is a type of "being true" in an ontological sense of selfhood, an ontological commitment, "the assurance—the credence and the trust—of existing in the mode of self-hood."[11] The opposite is the notion of episteme, of science, in the sense of ultimate and self-founding knowledge.[12] Attestation lends itself to a truth of another order than the test of verification and falsification.[13] The question of veracity, distinct from questions of truth, stems from attestation and attestation is better suited to questions of selfhood than descriptions of self. The criterion of truth that applies to description does not apply to the veracity of a declaration of intention or sincerity of intention which is attestation. One attests to one's intentional aim.

Section 2: *Idem* and *Ipse*

The second major feature of Ricoeur's hermeneutics of self is the separation of two distinct senses of identity—*idem* from *ipse*. One of the most central questions in *Oneself as Another* is, is there a sense of self which is permanent in time? Though there is a zone of overlapping, *idem* (sameness) and *ipse* (self) are not synonymous. Ricoeur lists four types of sameness (*idem*): numerical identity, extreme resemblance, uninterrupted continuity, and permanence over time. As we shall see later, it is this last type of sameness, permanence over time, that houses the intersection between *idem* and *ipse*. Let me first briefly describe what is meant by these types of sameness.

1. Numerical identity means that the number of times something happens does not affect its identity. An example is that a cup is the same cup no matter how many times I use it. The opposite of numerical identity is plurality.
2. Extreme resemblance simply means extreme similarity. Twins are an example. The opposite of extreme resemblance is difference.
3. Uninterrupted continuity means that although a thing may change over time it is the same being by virtue of the continuity among its successive states. In this sense a tree is the same tree all the while it goes through the cycles of the four seasons. The implication is that although a thing may be altered with time, the change is pre-determined by the thing itself. The opposite of uninterrupted continuity is discontinuity.
4. Permanence in time means that even though aspects of the thing have changed, the thing remains itself. Ricoeur's example is that of the structure of a tool that has had all its parts replaced. The structure is favored over the event. The structure of the tool is the same even it all the parts are different from the original parts.

While these four senses of sameness apply to the notion of personal identity, they cannot be considered alone.

Now, Ricoeur wants to distinguish these four senses or uses of sameness (*idem*) from identity as self (*ipse*). The distinction between *idem* and *ipse* is important because it enables a subjectivity that is permanent in time. It is in the process of narrative mediation of these two senses of identity that narrative identity is created. Ricoeur asks his readers to conceptualize the following diagram:

Idem<————————> NARRATIVE IDENTITY< ————————>*Ipse*

same   self

character   promise

Under the pole on the left are the words "same," "*idem*," and "character." Under the pole on the right are "self," "*ipse*," and "promise."

There are two models with which to answer the question that began the discussion of narrative identity: Does permanence in time have anything to do with personal identity?[14] The two models are represented by "character" and "promise." Character is identity as sameness or identity as permanent defining characteristics. This is not the common usage of character in the sense that there is no ethical content here. And the second model is defined by the act of keeping a promise, which is a very different sense of sameness over time. The model that consistency of commitment over time evidences, assumes that one's convictions or projects have been challenged by the passing of time but that a person with this sense of identity decides to honor her commitments nonetheless.

Let me explain. At one pole there is character which includes all the qualities of sameness listed before (numerical identity, extreme similarity, uninterrupted development and permanence in time). Character, here, is understood as the distinctive marks which permit the re-identification of a human individual as the same individual over time.[15] Character designates the set of lasting dispositions by which a person is recognized. The specific lasting dispositions that character designates are habit and acquired definitions. Each habit formed and sedimented constitutes a character trait.

So, character as Ricoeur defines it means sameness as a result of not changing essentially. His conception of commitment is different. For example, when one keeps a promise, it is assumed that the values, priorities, and projects of a person may have changed but—and this is an important distinction—the person decides to honor the promise, in spite of the changes, for ethical reasons. What ethical reasons? We are told at once that they are self evident and that two of the reasons are "the obligation to safeguard the institution of language" and "to respond to the trust that others put in my faithfulness."[16] Ricoeur puts a lot of weight on this point. Keeping a promise "does indeed appear to stand as a challenge to time, a denial of change."[17]

So, Ricoeur wants to argue that there is a difference between character as defined above the constancy of self evidenced by the act of keeping a promise. And this difference is an ethical one. The ethical difference gives rise to a type of consistent identity, an identity which has a permanence in time different from the permanence of "character" (lasting dispositions).

keeping one's promise . . . does indeed appear to stand as a challenge to time, a denial of change: even if my desire where to change my opinion or inclination, 'I will hold firm'[18]

The person who keeps a promise has a different type of identity than the person with "character," because the person who has character has unintentionally remained the same over time and has therefore maintained the same (*idem*) identity over time, while the promise keeper has intentionally decided to remain the same (*ipse*), in some important sense, even though she has undergone change. These are not mutually exclusive categories but they are different senses of identity. The *ethical* decision that results from the challenge to the identity of the promise keeper (the challenge posed by shifts in values and commitments) is a decision to favor consistency over flux. The difference in ethical quality between *ipse* and *idem*, between the act of keeping a promise and "character," is the intentional element.

By constructing a polar opposition between self-consistency and character, I wanted to highlight the properly ethical dimension of selfhood, irrespective of the perpetuation of character . . . narrative identity makes the two ends of the chain link up with one another: the permanence in time of character and that of self-constancy.[19]

Section 3: Otherness

The first half of *Oneself as Another* asked the question "who?" Who is speaking? Who is acting? Who is telling her story? The second part of the project introduces a new question, who is the moral subject? The moral subject turns out to be the one who has ethical intention.

Ricoeur defined "ethical intention" as "aiming at the 'good life,' with and for others, in just institutions."[20] Let me explain these three components in turn. The first component of ethical intention is aiming at the good life. To this end, "Life-plans" are developed which stem from moving back and forth between abstract ideas and the weighing of the advantages and disadvantages of a life-plan on the level of practice. "Action-configurations" occur as one considers and acts upon various particulars that are one part of the whole life plan. It is a specific and particular action that aims at something larger. It aims at a life-plan. The concept of the life plan enables Ricoeur to establish an answer to the old question, how can we simultaneously maintain that each act should be an "end in itself" and also that each act tends toward an "ultimate end?" An action-figuration is an end in itself *and* because action-figurations stem from life-plans taken together, they tend toward the large life-plan or "ultimate end." While the notion of the life-plan accentuates the voluntary, even willful, side of the existential project, the notion of narrative unity accentuates the organization of causes and chance with intention and desire. From the onset the person is the subject of suffering as much as acting. Narrating is a technique of appropriation. Narrative unity is concordant discordance; it is a technique for holding together (more accurately, juggling) voluntary and involuntary conditions and events together in a way that "makes sense."

The re-introduction of the hermeneutical point of view is necessitated by the "back-and-forth motion" between the ideal of the good life and particular life choices. This relationship is like a reader's relationship to a text in which the whole and parts are to be understood in terms of each other. The good life is that life in which actions are both ends in themselves and are also directed toward actualizing particular ideas. The process of mediating what is best for one's life as a whole and particular preferences and practices requires ongoing acts of interpretation —interpretation of the self and interpretation of action.

Of course, the process of making practical judgments often provokes a conflict of interpretations. One associated problem is that the process of mediating between practical decisions and the ideal of the good life is not subject to observational verification. One must make practical decisions in the present which bring one closer to the idea. But in practice this is not easy. It becomes the problem of seeing the forest through the trees. it is here that attestation comes in. Recall that attestation is a type of testimony which has credence and invokes trust from the listener. The trust it invokes has to do with the sincerity of the speaker. Attestation is testimony based on conviction that one is existing, being in an ontological mode, that is "true to oneself." From this ontological mode one is able to make decisions that are both ends in themselves and lead to an ideal.

Now how does the second part of the ethical aim, what Ricoeur calls "solicitude," link up with the first part? Recall that the ethical aim was defined as aiming at the good life with and for others in just institutions. Solicitude is the second aspect—with and for others. Solicitude is the mutual exchange of self esteem.[21] The self is worthy of esteem, not by reason of accomplishments, but by reason of its capacities. This is capacity in the sense of Merleau-Ponty's "I can" extended from the physical to the ethical. I am that being who can evaluate her actions and the one who assesses practical decisions in relation to my vision of the good life. The "I can" of being-able-to-do corresponds on the ethical plane to being-able-to-judge.

But others play a mediating role between capacities and realization. Ricoeur returns to Aristotle's conception of friendship and its role as a transition between the solitary virtue of the aim of the good life and a virtue belonging to the political sphere—justice. For Aristotle, friendship is not simply a feeling of affection or attachment to others, it is an ethical activity. Friendship is a virtue. Of the distinctions between three types of friendship: friendship for the sake of good, for the sake of utility, or for pleasure, the first type of friendship is preferred because it implies mutual generosity and reciprocity. According to the ideal of mutuality each loves the other for what she is rather than for advantage or pleasure. When self-esteem, together they achieve the second part of the ethical aim. Solicitude is the exchange of self-esteem among friends. This mutual reciprocal exchange of self-esteems is the way other persons enter into the aim of the good life. "Being-as" should be constitutive of this kind of mutuality.

The third component of the ethical intention ("just institutions") involves a modality of obligation, of responsibility. Ricoeur is interested in grounding the third part of the good life (institutional environment) in something other than the idea of justice. He argues that the autonomy of the self develops dialogically as a result of obligations, by showing that the norm of respect owed to other persons is connected to the ethical aim. The respect owed to persons is to autonomy, on the moral plane, as solicitude is to the aim of the good life, on the ethical plane.[22]

The dialogic structure referred to above is a result of the fact that there are at least two people involved in the act of making and keeping a promise. Ricoeur argues that there is more at stake in one's fidelity to a promise made than personal integrity which results from inter-personal reciprocity. In fact, "the false promise is a figure of the evil of violence in the use of language."[23] Recall that for Ricoeur

> self-constancy through time (is) the highest expression of identity of *ipse* in contrast to that of *idem,* that is, in opposition to the mere permanence of perseverance of things (a permanence that is found on the plane of selfhood only in character).[24]

To apply the principle of being faithful to one's word is to apply the rule of reciprocity to language acts.

Now consider the ethical weight Ricoeur puts on the act of keeping a promise as contrasted with character, i.e., the distinction between *ipse* and *idem.* The morality of obligation is of interest as a type of "being in the self" distinguished earlier from a type of selfhood associated with character. Ricoeur goes on at some length to discuss the veil of promises not kept. His argument is that the individual becomes human only under conditions of certain institutions, in this case linguistic institutions. And the obligation to serve these institutions is itself a condition for the human agent to continue to develop.[25]

Ricoeur then extends the notion of solicitude as concerned with respect for the "otherness of persons" to *critical solicitude.* Critical solicitude is solicitude that has passed through the double test of moral conditions of respect and the conflicts generated by respect. This is an advanced stage of morality having to do with conflicts that arise on the way from moral rule to moral judgment in a particular situation. Having passed this test, critical solicitude is ultimately a form of practical wisdom appropriate to the arena of interpersonal relations.[26]

Part II: Narrative Criteria

Three issues will be addressed in this part of this chapter. First, I will argue that Ricoeur adopts and privileges a conception of narrative that assumes principles of classical aesthetics. Second, I will argue that the Aristotelian-based narrative theory Ricoeur develops in the three volumes of *Time and Narrative* is imported into his theory of narrative identity as conceived in *Oneself as Another*. This is to say that Ricoeur's understanding of identity is informed by his aesthetic preference. I will address the extent to which Ricoeur explicitly argues for these aesthetic principles in his theory of personal identity and the extent to which they are implicitly assumed. Third, I will argue that Ricoeur marginalizes alternative forms of narrative and identity, namely those structured around alternative principles.

The primary project of *Oneself as Another* is to show how the identity of the character is constructed in connection with the plot.[27] Ricoeur begins his discussion of Narrative Identity in *Oneself as Another* reviewing what he means by "emplotment" in *Time and Narrative*. He reminds readers that by concordance, he means the "principle of order" that presides over what Aristotle call "the arrangement of facts." And discordance is the same that it was in *Time and Narrative*, "the reversals of fortune that make the plot an ordered transformation from an initial situation to a terminal situation." And configuration is the "art of composition which mediates between concordance and discordance."[28]

The connection between poetic activity and temporal experience allows for a synthesizing of discordant experience. Aristotelian emplotment becomes the method of maintaining Augustine's three-fold present. Then Ricoeur wants to extend Aristotle's rules for the composition of tragedies (embellished with a temporal element) to the entire narrative field. The larger project of all three volumes of *Time and Narrative* is to "confirm the universal character of the formal principle of narrative configuration . . . the temporal synthesis of the heterogeneous."[29] And this classical model for holding together discontinuous fragmentary events should be the standard for "every composition we call narrative."[30] This configurational operation is transhistorical but not attemporal.[31]

The Aristotelian requirements of unity/wholeness, and that the imitation (understood by Ricoeur as *mimesis₂*) should be of actions rather than character or consciousness, are the basis for Ricoeur's understanding of discordant concordance and his insistence that narrative should have a singular dominant authorial voice. As regards the first requirement, that of unity and wholeness, Ricoeur says,

the one formal feature of the Aristotelian notion of *muthos* that has to be preserved, beyond its successive instantiations in genres (for example, tragedy or the novel) and types (for example, Elizabethan tragedy or the nineteenth-century novel) is the criterion of unity and completeness.[32]

And that which is "whole" and "complete" must have

> a beginning, a middle, and an end; that is, if the beginning introduces the middle, if the middle with its reversal and recognition scenes leads to the end, and if the end concludes the middle. Then the configuration wins out over the episodic form, concordance overcomes discordance.[33]

The "anti-closure" of a narrative "reaches the threshold beyond which we must exclude the work from the domain of art."[34] The other unacceptable narrative structure is "polyphonic" narrative which is opposed to monological (or homo-phonic) narrative. Narratives without a "single and unified authorial consciousness"[35] mark a "limit placed on composition in terms of levels, a limit beyond which any starting point in the notion of plot becomes unrecognizable."[36] In the monological novel the voice of the narrator-author establishes itself as a single voice "at the summit of the pyramid of voices."[37] Earlier on Ricoeur says, "I am calling narrative exactly what Aristotle calls *muthos,* the organization of events."[38] Configuration is the "art of composition which mediates between concordance and discordance."[39] This is a type of synthetic unity.

Structural unity and completeness are necessary but not sufficient conditions for Ricoeurean narration. Sufficient conditions are: temporal organization, homophony, monological structure, and the privileging of plot over character, actions or thoughts.

Identity of a character makes sense only in relation to plot, more specifically, in relation to the wholeness and unity of the plot. In this way actions have meaning in relation to structure. Identity is possible only within the limits set by the plot. The characters internalize the plot; they are thereby "emplotted" to use Ricoeur's terms. A character's identity is dynamic only to the extent, and in the manner, consistent with the narrative.[40]

> It is indeed in the story recounted, with its qualities of unity, internal structure, and completeness which are conferred by emplotment, that the character preserves throughout the story an identity correlative to that of the story itself . . . the identity of the character is comprehensible through the transfer to the character of the operation of emplotment.[41]

The function of narration is to artificially order discordant experience by emplotting it. Narrative is the concordant structure within which discordant events are assimilated. The primary difference between narrative configuration and the sort of connectedness claimed by impersonal description rests in the status of event. Description tells of discordant events. But in the narrative model, the event is discordant to the extent that it "springs up." However, once it is assimilated narratively it becomes another stage in the advancing plot. Narration ties events together. "If my life cannot be grasped as a singular totality, I could never hope it to be successful, complete."[42] As always in Ricoeur, the reciprocal constitution of action and the self is assumed, "by narrating a life of which I am not author as to existence, I make myself co-author as to its meaning."[43]

The answer to the question which guides this inquiry, the question "who?," rests on Ricoeur's conception of Narrative Identity. Narrative Identity is his solution to the problem of consistent subjectivity in the face of flux. It is the answer to the question "In what sense am I the same person that I was years ago when my values, projects, and goals were completely different?" The changes which take place in the subject are accounted for, and controlled by, the plot. We act and intend in accordance with plot and in this sense we each have narrative identities. In light of this assertion, it is significant that Ricoeur insists that only certain particular types of constructions are properly termed "plots."

Ricoeurean criteria for structural form exclude from the category of narrative any story that lacks a whole and unified configuration; a story must have a beginning which leads to a middle, and a middle with recognitions and reversals which necessitates a conclusion. A narrative must not be open-ended. The "anti-closure" of a narrative is enough to have it excluded from the realm of art, according to Ricoeur.[44] And a narrative must have a Master-voice and Master-consciousness, "The co-existence of dominant voices," Ricoeur insists, "cannot form the structure of a narration."[45] Dialogical form, for example, violates the criterion of Master-voice. Narratives which are dialogic, "designate a limit placed on composition . . . beyond which my starting point in the notion of plot becomes unrecognizable."[46] Ricoeur stresses the "unified viewpoint" unproblematically. Texts which have a "plurality of centers of consciousness irreducible to a common denominator" refuse to be subject to "the organizing role of emplotment."[47]

If one's personal story were told in a form that does not fit these criteria (unity, wholeness, singular dominant authorial voice, monological structure) it would be considered description rather than narrative. Ricoeur distinguishes description from narration by saying that description simply articulates a chronology of events while narration, $mimesis_2$, organizes events temporally in order to give events meaning.

The three stages of *mimesis* are described as: $mimesis_1$, pre-figuration; $mimesis_2$, configuration; and $mimesis_3$, refiguration. $Mimesis_2$ is the type of *mimesis* that concerns us here; it is narrative configuration. It is at this stage of *mimesis* that the narrator re-figures events and actions. Recall also that in *Time and Narrative* Ricoeur's criticism of literary works which aim to establish the most exact correspondence to the reality they imitate is that these works are the result of a simple understanding of *mimesis*. This is a result of considering *mimesis* only in its crudest form, its first stage, its lowest function, description. $Mimesis_2$ is concordant discordance; it is a structural operation which synthesizes a variety of incidents into a unified and whole story. The art of configuration, composition, $mimesis_2$, is to grasp together incidences and events and represent them as causally connected, even necessary. Plot is the narrative structure that integrates and orders the multiplicity of experience. For Ricoeur, "the universal character of the formal principle of narrative configuration (is) the temporal synthesis of the heteroge-neous."[48]

If one's personal story does not fit the aesthetic criteria of *Time and Narrative* it would not be "narrative" and the narrative identity described in *Oneself as Another* would be impossible if there were no "narrative" for it to correspond to. One's narrative identity is formed in the process or attempt to synthesize discordant experience into this traditional form.

What does the identity of the narrator of a life-story told in an alternative structure look like from the Ricoeurean point of view? It looks precisely like the "dead" modern subject. In fact, Ricoeur clings so tightly to his aesthetic criteria precisely because he sees them as a solution to the postmodern denial of subjectivity in modern understanding. His claim is that narrative connection ties together the fractured self. And if it were not for the imposition of this structure on narrative, there would be nothing to differentiate it from the experiences of multiplicity, flux, and contingency. So, in order for narrative to serve its function it must do more than merely describe events (described earlier as a naive understanding of *mimesis*) or merely articulate a stream of thoughts as they happen. Narrative configures discordant life into a concordant structure.

Ricoeur seems to be afraid that if narratives are not structured in the way he mandates, then narratives will fall into a description of a chaotic mess of unrelated and meaningless experiences. But I am suggesting that there is a spacious middle ground between Ricoeurean narrative structure and a mere chronology of events. It is my thesis that there are narratives which do not fit either of these extreme categories and yet they serve the imperative identity functions—they privilege attestation or avowal, they provide a sense of the distinction between sameness and selfhood, and most importantly they assign meaning to experiences and actions and events.

Ricoeur laments the loss of the identity that corresponds to the crisis of traditional narrative configuration. Particularly troubling are some "unsettling cases" of contemporary novels which he terms "fictions of the loss of identity." These are narratives which deviate from the principles of Aristotelian aesthetics. These narratives do not aspire to the norm of unity, and the further they are from Ricoeur's ideal structure, the less coherent, intelligible, and ethical. Novels of this type "expose selfhood by taking away the support of sameness,"[49] so that the hero can no longer be identified with a set of lasting dispositions or commitments.

To counter Ricoeur in his own terms, my argument is that not only can a narrative concern itself with what the hero does between events,[50] alternative structures are available because they play with the very status of the "events" of traditional narratives and there is critical engagement with experiences that traditional narratives skip over. The liberalizing of narrative structure opens up richer possibilities for the re-association of meaning. I agree with Ricoeur that the structural function narrative serves is an intrinsic part of its unique capacity to construct meaning, but a broader and richer narrative structure than Ricoeur imagines would engender endless possibilities for meaning construction.

Narrative will still retain its strength in accounting for and creating identity without relying on a model which bases identity on a type of consistency over time. Narrative Identity Theory can retain its emphasis on linguistic attestation, and the distinction between selfhood and sameness, without aligning selfhood with the ethical commitment to challenge change. Ricoeur's attachment of the act of keeping a promise to both subjectivity in general and ethical subjectivity in particular, leaves no room for the change in self resulting from Ricoeur's own description of "second naivete" which follows critical reflection. The theoretical weight placed on intentional self consistency is incongruent with the kind of agency in which the result of critical reflection are manifest.

The ethical associations in Ricoeur's account of *ipse,* particularly the ethical associations, are problematic on several counts. First, it leaves no room for changes in commitment or changes in self resulting from changes in commitment. For example, Ricoeur says, "even if my desire were to change, even if I were to change my opinion or inclination, 'I will hold firm.' It is not necessary for the promise to be meaningful to keep one's word."[51] Second, Ricoeur insists that not only ethical selfhood but any sense of self is achieved by the commitment to honor one's past commitments *because* the commitment to honor one's commitments (a type of sincerity) is a denial of change. "Keeping one's promise does appear to stand as a challenge to time, a denial of change."[52] And this sincerity in denying changes brought by time is the crucial aspect of *ipse* selfhood. This is the opposite of sameness over time resulting from change *not* having occurred. This (*ipse*) is sameness over time resulting from the constant, and intentional ethical commitment to remain the same over time is an achievement in selfhood. Third, Ricoeur makes no mention, in this theory of narrative identity, of potential changes in commitment or actions that may result from gaining new information or from changes in external circumstances. In fact, it is this kind of external flux that consistency of self, evidenced by keeping a promise, is meant to combat.

The difficulty of locating a self that is permanent in time leads Ricoeur to the solution that is Narrative Identity Theory. One's narrative is created in the narrative rendering of the relationship between *ipse* and *idem.* His solution is that the self is that which is consistent with plot. The self is the same self who narrates a unified and whole narrative, with one dominant authorial voice and consciousness, over time. A self in this sense (*ipse*) may appear to have changed in the eyes of another, but if the other is cognizant of the narrative that the self is a part of, the other will acknowledge that the self changed only in accordance with the demands of plot.

But it seems to me to remain true that one's actions make sense only in the context of one's story even if the story is *not* structured in the Ricoeurean style. To tell one's story is to assign meaning to events and experiences; and re-telling one's story is a way to creatively re-assign meaning to experience after critical reflection. Our modern understanding of self-narrative since Rousseau has been that to narrate one's story is to co-author the very self doing the narrating; redescription involves a reconstitution of self. I am claiming that narrating *is itself* a process of structuring experience even when the structure is not unified/whole, discordant/concordant.

In the second and third chapters I will examine one example of an alternative emplotment. In the forth and fifth chapters I will argue that alternative narratives are at least as effective as traditional narratives in providing experience with meaning, in appropriating the involuntary. In fact, it is Ricoeur's conservative aesthetic which leaves his theory of personal identity incomplete in such a way that certain conceptions of self are not recognized. I will argue that these alternative narratives, and the selves they engender, are as complete and ethical as those Ricoeur identifies.

I assume along with Ricoeur that refiguration occurs in the life and actions of the emplotted subject. But beyond theory, I wonder what results alternative structures could have on future actions of emplotted subjects. Our reading of fiction has made narrative beginnings and endings familiar to us so that we should be able to "stabilize" them in real life. For decades many feminist literary critics have assumed a narrative identity theory similar to Ricoeur's and have argued that traditionally assumed "universal" plots, the "quest plot" for example, are not universal but male plots[53] and that women must both retrieve and reinterpret old plots and create new ones.[54] Women have long been encouraged to abandon "the marriage plot"[55] or the "victim plot"[56] or the "Freudian master-plot"[57] in favor of alternative plots, but I am arguing something further: assuming that narrative structure affects action and identity, narrative choice should include not only alternative plots in terms of content but also alternative formal structures. This means that narrative agency can take on entirely new meaning if not only the content of stories is altered but the form in which they are told is also altered.

Ricoeur would agree with the narrator who says that we live our lives by telling stories and that these internal re-constructions determine action, and that,

> were a complete inventory to be undertaken I think that we would find that our entire stock of story forms is quite manageably small, countable in single digits . . . our human creativity is . . . exercised not in the production of new forms but rather in the finding of ways to force our material into the finite available few. We trim off and discard into forgetfulness the incoherent bits that won't go into any kind of story we can tell ourselves—incoherent *because* they won't go in; that is, if we notice them at all.[58]

There is something further that Ricoeur does not account for—something that will be the focus of chapter five. If, as he suggests, narrative will form the "yet untold stories of our lives,"[59] the problem is that "The aesthetic preference for wholeness will often lead us to actions we would not otherwise undertake." (Rebecca Goldstein, *The Late Summer Passion of a Woman of Mind*).[60]

Chapter II

Fault Lines

In our treatment of narrative identity, we observed that it is the virtue of the narrative to join together agents and patients in the entangling of multiple life histories. But we must go further and take into account more deeply concealed forms of suffering: the incapacity to tell a story, the refusal to recount, the insistence of the untellable—phenomena that go beyond mishaps and adventures, which can always be made meaningful through the strategy of emplotment.[1]

The problem with what Ricoeur says here is that the extent to which narrative makes these phenomena meaningful is limited by the structure of the very thing that performs this sense-making function; potentially meaningful experience will be left out of a unified and whole plot structure of the very thing that performs this sense-making function; potentially meaningful experience will be left out of a unified and whole plot structure if it is anomalous or if it cannot be synthesized. Experience becomes dichotomized as meaningful or trivial, anomaly or pattern, and then is either synthesized or silenced. But even experience that is silenced or repressed is potentially meaningful in a plot that is not unified and whole.

The discordant/concordant feature of Ricoeurean narratives deals with anomalous experience, or experience between "events," in one of two ways. Either the experience is forgotten, repressed, trivialized, so that it does not enter into the narrative (As Ricoeur says in *Time and Narrative,* "we do not ask what the hero did between episodes"[2]) or such experiences can *become* the narrative. An example of the first method is that we do not know when Oedipus brushed his teeth. Even Aristotle's own example of the most well laid plot, Sophocles' *Oedipus Rex,* does not allow just any experience to enter the narrative. All the experiences that take place between events, anomalous experience, and the breaks in continuous experience, are discordant or heterogeneous, according to Ricoeur. These types of experiences are "synthesized" to fit Aristotelian formal structure. For Ricoeur, narrative *is* the "synthesis of the heterogeneous."

In regard to the second method, a reader may ask: Doesn't the Ricoeurean model allow for experiential rupture to be the content of the story? Cannot one's experience of fracture and discontinuity be what the story is *about*, or part of what the story is about? In other words, isn't making a story in which change is interpreted as continuity a Ricoeurean move? My reply is that on the Ricoeurean model, a story about these types of experiences would still be structured like the whole/unified Aristotelian plot. This means that these experiences would be synthesized by its structure. Even such a story (a story with change interpreted as continuity) must be transformed into Aristotelian formal structure in order to be a "narrative" according to Ricoeur's model.

One way narrative can synthesize discordant experience is by constructing causal connections. For example, let us say that one's narrative was about the quest to become a great composer, and then a sudden illness results in deafness, and even then this narrator goes on to become a great composer. One way to make sense of the senselessness of this debilitating illness is to narrate it as the *cause* of the success as a composer. In order to make sense of the senseless, the anomalous, the accidental, or the involuntary, a Ricoeurean narrator will either drop events from the narrative (as Sophocles did) or the narrator will synthesize the material and one method of synthesis is the construction of causal connections. Ricoeur's point is exactly this: an accident, or anomaly, or rupture in continuous experience, would be understood differently if it were assimilated. Assimilation is a sense-making function.

But Meena Alexander in her memoir *Fault Lines,* addresses this point and raises an interesting and important objection. If she told a story that made change and discontinuity what the story was *about* she would become *only* those experiences of rupture because all else would be synthesized by classical structure. Those experiences of radical cultural dislocation, for example, would *be* the story. Then she would have a "narrative" according to Ricoeur, but Alexander wants her narrative, her identity, to be more than a collection of fault lines, "more than a crack in the earth marking boundaries." Further, some types of experience are more difficult to synthesize than others and some people have more of these types of experiences than others. Cross-cultural experience, for example, is more difficult to synthesize.

How does one synthesize culturally incommensurable stories? An eighty-year-old widow in India will experience, perhaps for the first time in her life, a degree of self-direction after her husband's death. This may well be the first time she makes decisions for herself, the first time she chooses how to spend her time. This is a time for life that Indian women often look forward to. At this age a woman is the most powerful figure in the family. She can choose the careers of her children and grandchildren. She will determine rituals around the home; she will decide everything from when the family eats to when they go to sleep. Previously all these things would have been determined by her husband or before that by *his* mother. The story of an eight-year-old widow in America is quite different. The elderly American woman will probably have less, not more, self-direction and influence and connectedness with her family. In America age is fended off; it is not something one looks forward to. Now for an elderly woman who lives in *both* cultures to tell a unified narrative would be very structurally demanding. It would require more negation of experience than it would of an elderly woman who lives in one culture or the other. It is in this sense that intercultural narrative conflict will be more structurally demanding than intracultural conflict.

There is another problem; the way in which Ricoeurean narrative theory makes sense of the "unsayable" is not adequately theorized. In fact, the quote from Ricoeur with which I began this chapter is the only place where there is any reference at all to the incapacity to tell a story, refusal to recount, or insistence on the untellable. My claim is that the incapacity to tell a story may well be the *result* of the requirement to tell the story in a certain way. The "unsayable" is that which is silenced, repressed, marginalized by Ricoeur's aesthetic requirements. In other words, Ricoeur's structural requirements make certain stories difficult to tell.

My argument is that it is precisely these aesthetic criteria, that inform Ricoeur's conception of identity, that *create* narrative difficulty. Since Ricoeur does not address this issue, but rather insists on the universality of Aristotelian plot structure, one is left to assume that "deeper forms of suffering" will be subjected to the same authoritarian regulatory practices. The aesthetic criteria for the form in which the story is told do not take into account the "incapacity to tell a story." The "untell-able" is not theoretically connected to emplotment, far less, "made meaningful" by strategic emplotment. In fact, as I will argue in later chapters, these aesthetic criteria *contribute* to the "incapacity to tell a story."

The life of Meena Alexander, a contemporary poet, exemplifies these problems. She experiences more than just the garden variety narrative conflict theorized so completely by Western feminist theorists.[3] She embodies the conflict of radically different cultural traditions. Her struggles begin with trying to find a decolonized voice in which to narrate. Then the Ricoeurean practice of synthesizing heterogeneous experience is particularly difficult for her because her experiences are culturally and linguistically heterogeneous. And Alexander is not the only one with this type of problem. She is a member of an increasingly large group of theorists who focus on the issues of cross-cultural conflict, physical dislocation, and experiential rupture, in the formation of subjectivity.

In this chapter I hope to accomplish two tasks. In the first section, I will take a brief detour through the theoretical home of Alexander's narrative practice, by looking at some aspects of the work of Gayatri Spivak, Judith Butler, Nita Kumar, and Rosi Braidotti. I choose to concentrate on these particular theorists for very specific reasons. Each of these theorists provides a sketch, a figuration, of a form of subjectivity which is an alternative to the modern Western conception of the Enlightenment subject (epitomized by the Locke, Descartes, and Kant) which focuses on reason as a central human capacity while marginalizing non-rational (for example unconscious) aspects of subjectivity.[4] Nor are these the "dead" or "fractured" postmodern subjects of Barthes or Foucault. Moreover, these figurations are not even modeled on the classical aesthetic of Ricoeur's subject. These figurations are alternative to what Ricoeur considers his solution, or mediation of the gulf between the Enlightenment view of subjectivity and the postmodern denial of it. I call these alternative figurations of subjectivity the "theoretical home of Alexander's narrative practice" because each of them come about as a result of cultural dislocation and the subversion of regulatory or colonial discursive practices. Gayatri Spivak has offered the post-colonial subject, Judith Butler performative subjectivity, Nita Kumar the South Asian anticolonial subalternist subject, and Rosi Braidotti the nomadic subject. I would like to look to these four conceptions of subjectivity. Specifically, I will look to the *practices* of these types of subjects.

The second part of this chapter will move away from the theoretical to an illustrative example of the problems of identity associated with narrating within the limits of Ricoeurean structure, by focusing on the narrative of Meena Alexander's memoir *Fault Lines*. *Fault Lines* presents a narrative solution, a practical solution, to the problems associated with constant identity in the face of flux, contingency, and dislocation—a solution with an alternative to Ricoeur's structure.

Part I: Alternative Figurations

The construction of Gayatri Spivak's collective subject begins with the "unlearning" of "authoritarian fictions" of the self. She responds to the regulatory function of such fictions in the assignment of meaning to experience by "unlearning." "Unlearning" is the beginning, a preliminary conceptual step which involves understanding one's privilege as one's loss. In other words, the slave has certain knowledge that the master does not. Understanding this means understanding that one's privileged position makes other knowledge inaccessible. Other knowledge in this sense means marginalized knowledge, for example, subaltern knowledges. Subalterns may, for example, develop subtle nuanced methods of self-expression which are undetectable by those with power as undetectability may be a requirement of survival. Authoritarian fictions are fictions which narrate ethical and political conflict metaphysically. This means representing ethical or political values and motives as "natural" or just "the way things are." Unlearning involves recognizing the repressive construction of what presents itself as obvious, free, or natural.

Spivak is interested in uncovering the strategies that authoritarian fictions use to "solve" conflicts by the imposition of power. This is the second step, the deconstructive step. She insists that deconstruction is not so much the exposing of error as it is the constant and persistent questioning of the production of truths, and she takes from Derrida the idea that interruption of text disrupts the "so-called" unity of voice and intention. The interest here is in focusing on the itinerary of authoritarian fictions so as to call into question the "complacent apathy of self-centralization."[5] She wants to think of the decolonialized autobiographical subject as a communal subject. The identity of the subject is consistent with the identity of the place/space/culture in which it exists. Identity is completely contextualized. Rather than individuation, a central aspect of identity as Spivak understands it is its embeddedness in a time, a place, a context. Spivak maintains that one of the most essential tasks of the critical reader is to ask "what subject-effects were systemically effaced and trained to efface themselves so that a canonic norm might emerge?"[6]

Now, Spivak's next question is how can one narrate one's life while speaking the language of the colonizer? In order to answer this question she explores the nature of the relationship between autobiographical "identity" and the autobiography which is (to the extent that it can be) decolonized. As one might expect, Spivak aligns the autobiographical identity formed in authoritative fictions with the canon, with the learned, powerful, and effacing. Decolonized autobiography comes about as a result of a learned (or unlearned) perspective. This is a narrative which begins by unlearning privilege, then deconstructs normative values in search of the power structures which support them, and then engages in "new narrativations of older scripts."[7]

Spivak's comparison of the Latin *idem* and Sanskrit *idam* (both mean "same") and the Latin *ipse* and the Sanskrit *aham* will prove important to an alternative understanding of identity. (This is more precisely *idamvada* and *ahamvada*). Recall that in Ricoeur's reading *idem* is demonstrated by distinguishing characteristics over time. *Idem* is Ricoeur's "character" as opposed to the self-sameness demonstrated by keeping a promise (*ipse*). But the Sanskrit *idam* is not understood as sameness in the same sense. *Idam* does not denote unique characteristics which make the thing (the person or the object) the same thing over time; rather, it has to do with what is *not* unique.[8] *Idam* means sameness in multiplicity, "in the sense of multitudes or repetitions."[9] In other words, this *idam* is not associated with personal identity, as is *idem*, but is rather the opposite. It is not unique personal identity but an identity of like things.

Spivak considers her job as a deconstructionist to be to "shake the stakes" of egoism (*ipse* or *ahem*) so as to reveal *idam*.[10] This distinction is crucial to understanding Spivak's conception of identity. She insists that we should cease thinking of ourselves and our opinions as at the center of our own self-possession: "alternative storytelling doesn't give you an identity if you think of identity as something intimately personal which lets you know who you are. It gives you a whole field of representation within which something like an 'identity' can be represented as a basis for agency."[11]

Spivak's embodied subject is neither essential nor biologically determined. Embodied subjectivity has to do with one's situation, location, in the world. Spivak is Ricoeurean when she insists that, "what we call experience is a staging of experience"[12] and that the job of intellectuals is to offer accounts of the mechanisms of staging.[13] This "staging" is what Ricoeur calls the "synthetic" nature of experience. And one of the primary mechanisms of that staging is emplotment in the classical structure. But while Ricoeur promotes proficiency in these mechanisms so as to better stage, or synthesize, experience, Spivak suggests that we know these mechanisms well enough. In fact, we know them so well that authoritarian modes of holding experience together seem natural to us rather than artificial. Ricoeur's foundational aesthetic privileges an authoritarian fiction of precisely the type that Spivak suggests should be unlearned. The chapters which follow will not only answer Spivak's question about who is "systematically effaced and trained to efface themselves so that a canonical norm might emerge?" they will also inquire into the mechanisms of this effacement.

Judith Butler[14] is also interested in these mechanisms or what she terms "regulatory practices" which constitute identity, the internal coherence of the subject, the self-identical status of a person. Like Spivak, Butler asks, "To what extent is unity a normative ideal rather than a descriptive feature of experience?"[15] While Ricoeur's account, and many accounts of personal identity, focus on internal elements of a person that are continuous and establish the self-identity of a person over time (like distinguishing characteristics or commitment not to change) Butler argues that the "coherence" and "continuity" of the "person" are not intrinsic features of personhood, but rather socially instituted and maintained norms of intelligibility.[16] And that "political construction of the subject proceeds with certain legitimizing and exclusionary aims."[17] Identity is an effect of power relations and Butler and Spivak both insist that a central question that must be asked is, who is excluded for identity categories and how is the exclusion maintained?

Butler calls the nature of identity "fictive" in the sense that it is created by practices rather than being a thing that exists independent of those practices. Identity is the effect of the repetition of regulatory practices and discourses like synthesizing discordant experiences to fit Aristotelian plot structure. But Butler calls for de-regulation, insisting that if repetition is bound to persist as the mechanism of the cultural reproduction of identities, then the crucial question is, "What kind of subversive repetition might call into question the regulatory practice of identity itself."[18] An example of one of Butler's answers to that question is the repetition of so-called heterosexual conventions in homosexual contexts. The performance of "butch" and "femme" roles, for example, parody performances of these roles in heterosexual contexts and expose the "utterly constructed status of the so-called heterosexual original. Thus gay is to straight *not* as copy is to original, but, rather, as copy is to copy."[19]

What Spivak calls "authoritarian fictions," Butler calls "regulatory fictions" of identity. These fictions are the place to begin disruption, and she looks to psychoanalytic accounts for critical strategies and sources of subversion.

In *Gender Trouble: Feminism and the Subversion of Identity*, Butler exposes the coercive and limiting consequences of identity categories and destabilizes identity constructions by exposing their normative regulative functions. The first step is to become aware of the ways in which we repeat and perform our identities. The second step is to become aware of the ways in which we repeat and perform our identities. The second step is the deconstructive one. Then she reconceptualizes identity and thinks of it instead as performance. Identity is performance as it is produced and re-produced by the regulatory practices of coherence. It is created in the process of performing it. Identity is performative in the sense that it constitutes the identity it is purported to be: "Identity is performatively constituted by the very 'expressions' of gender said to be its result."[20] So, for example, identity categories of gender are constructed by repetitive practices which are often thought of as the *results* of these categories. This repetitive performance not only constructs but also regulates other performances. Because this regulated repetition of gender categories is bound to persist, Butler promotes the subversive practice of parodic repetition.

Butler is interested in proliferating the possibilities for identity performance. Acknowledgment of various types of identity will involve the acknowledgment that there are different identities at different points in time. Certain *practices* create local and temporally particular identities and these practices, like the identities they create, are situated and contingent. Butler says, "My argument is that there need not be a 'doer behind the deed,' but that the 'doer' is variably constructed in and through the deed."[21]

This is not an existential theory of self as constituted through acts, rather, "It is precisely the discursively variable construction of each (self and acts) in and through the other."[22] that interests Butler. So, it follows that rather than trying to posit a primary identity as a foundation for political action, Butler thinks feminist theory should instead concern itself with the political possibilities that are a consequence of a radical critique of identity. In other words, there does not have to be an identity in place before its interests can be elaborated and in order for political action to be taken on the basis of those interests. In fact, the attempt to locate a common identity as the foundation for feminist politics precludes a radical critique of the political construction and regulation of identity.

Ricoeur agrees with Butler that the coherence and continuity of the subject are not features of experience, but are rather "socially instituted and maintained norms of intelligibility." But while Ricoeur's account of personal identity emphasizes sameness through time, continuity, and commitment to challenge change, Butler undermines the very practices that constitute internal coherence. Ricoeurean "rule-governed identity"[23] is the type of identity that "relies on the consistent and repeated invocation of rules that condition and restrict culturally intelligible practices of identity."[24] Butler's project is very *un*Ricoeurean since,

> the very notion of "the person" is called into question by the cultural emergence of those 'incoherent' or 'discontinuous' gendered beings who appear to be persons but who fail to conform to the gendered norms of cultural intelligibility by which persons are defined. The specters of discontinuity and incoherence . . . are

constantly prohibited and produced by the very laws that seek to establish causal or expressive lines of connection.[25]

"Intelligible" gender identities, for example, are those which in some way maintain continuity between sex, gender, sexual practice, and desire. "Unintelligible" gender identities do not maintain this continuity.

Butler is interested in exploring a type of agency that is not completely determined by culture and discourse. And in so doing she argues against two common faulty assumptions. First is the assumption that identity can only be established by recourse to a previously established "I." Second is the mistaken assumption that to be constituted by discourse is to be determined by discourse, where determination makes agency impossible.[26] Butler argues that the subject is not determined by the rules through which it is generated. The issue of agency is reformulated as a question of how signification and re-signification work. Identity is an *effect* of signification and there are rules concerning signification which restrict culturally intelligible practices of identity. "Intelligible" subjects are the effects of rule-based signifying practices and these rules operate through repetition. But signifying rules and practices conceal their own workings and naturalize their effects.

> because signification is not a founding act, but rather a regulated process of repetition . . . 'agency,' then, is to be located within the possibility of a variation on that repetition . . . it is only within the practices of repetitive signifying that a subversion of identity becomes possible.[27]

The reconceptualization of identity as an effect, as produced and generated, opens up new possibilities for agency, possibilities that are closed by positions that consider identity fixed and foundational. For identity to be an effect means that it is neither determined nor fully artificial and arbitrary: "construction is not opposed to agency; it is the necessary scene of agency." The critical task is . . . to locate strategies of subversive repetition enabled by those constructions."[28] Butler's inquiry attempts to locate the political in the very signifying practices that construct identity; she reformulates the question of agency as a question of how signification and resignification work.

Good examples of subversive signifying practices that construct identity are to be found in Nita Kumar's *Women as Subjects*.[29] This is a collection of the empirical data of field work in India. The studies are anthropological, sociological, historical, and there is also discursive textual analysis. Kumar is interested in finding out about the ways in which South Asian, postcolonial, female subjects can provide alternative paradigms for the process of constructing lives. Her method is to look at the hidden subversive ways in which these women "exercise agency even while outwardly part of a repressive normative order"[30] by uncovering subversive discourses, deviant practices, hidden uses of symbols, as subaltern methods of struggle toward the construction of identity in radical yet little recognized ways. The protest of the subjects in these studies does not take the recognized form; rather, it appears in activities of daily life. It appears in evasive tactics like countercultures of language, myths with double entendres, and diary writing. The essays show how subjectivity gets constituted by the articulation of alternative perspectives.

Several essays in Kumar's collection focus their analysis on alternative discourses expressed through song and story. "The subject that emerges is one that resists by fashioning her own discourse."[31] One article suggests that subjects existing between different social/cultural backgrounds and historical identities, exist in a space, a fault line, between two authoritarian influences, within which they can assert agency in co-constructing the self. These subjects are "discontinuous and apparently contradictory, not consistent, unified, or freely choosing, but a palimpsest of identities, constituted and reconstituted, constantly in flux."[32] The subject that emerges from Kumar's account is one which, like Butler's figuration, is fashioned by discourse, but is not a passive recipient of it, "even when the terms of discourse seem unchanged, the slight displacement of a symbol from its conventional positioning is enough to codify completely different, opposing meanings for the subject."[33] Obviously a sensitivity to the use of symbols is imperative in considering the manifestation of this type of discursive and metaphorical agency.

Kumar is not interested in positing a female subject that would replace the modern male subject. She does not want to resurrect the Cartesian subject or reconceptualize it; hers is a radical departure from it. Her approach is anti-colonial, subalternist, and South Asian at once. She prefers the term anti-colonial to "postcolonialism" as the later posits a system in which the inequity of power relations creates a totally passive object. Her approach is subalternist in the sense that it seeks to reinstate people without apparent power. And her approach is South Asian in the sense that before she goes about questioning the masculine subjectivity of the Enlightenment or overthrowing hierarchical dichotomies, she asks prior questions—questions about South Asian reality. For example, she asks if there has been a Modernism in South Asia comparable to the European one? Is the normative of South Asian history clearly masculine? And is masculinity itself characterized by rationality, independence, freedom, and action, as it is in the West? She looks to the empirical data of anthropological field work, and to myths, folktales, literature, and psychoanalytic data, all of which suggest that the dichotomies such as body/spirit, mind/matter, inside/outside, male/female, are "less rigorously constructed than in the West."[34] She finds a radically un-Cartesian assumption governing much Indian thought—that the world is fundamentally one. And she finds that there is not such a clearly delineated normative male subject and that the unitary qualities of Western man's rationality are not privileged. Nor do masculinity or femininity bear the same characteristics as they do in the West, nor do they have the same relationship to one another.

Unlike Ricoeur's conception of a narrative subject who constructs herself by organizing her experience in accordance with the tacitly assumed principles of classical aesthetics, the subjects of these field studies construct themselves in the process of subverting authoritarian modes of self-representation. The identities of these subjects are not inscribed by a text; their agency is exercised in the margins and the fault lines between dominant discourses.

Another alternative form of subjectivity with a strong linguistic dimension is Rosi Braidotti's "figuration" of the nomadic subject. The "nomad" practices an aesthetic style which reflects the arbitrary nature of the "identity" she deals with. Writing for the nomadic subject is,

> a process of undoing the illusory stability of fixed identities, bursting open the bubble of ontological security that comes with familiarity with one linguistic site. . . . Writing in this mode is about disengaging the sedentary nature of words, destabilizing commonsensical meanings, deconstructing established forms of consciousness.[35]

Braidotti's nomadism is akin to Fourcault's "countermemory." It is a form of resisting assimilation into dominant ways of representing the self.[36] "Nomadic shifts designate . . . a creative sort of becoming; a performative metaphor that allows for otherwise unlikely encounters and unsuspected sources of interaction of experience and knowledge."[37] Responding to contemporary theories of subjectivity like Ricoeur's, she suggests developing nomadic consciousness which requires the possession of a sense of identity that rests not on fixity but on contingency. It denies "authentic" identities or original sites of identity. Nomadic consciousness combines coherence with mobility. "It aims to rethink the unity of the subject"[38] that Ricoeur insists upon. Her work attempts to deconstruct what Ricoeur calls the "configurational competence" of the narrator.

> I am struck by the violence of the gesture that binds a fractured self to the performative illusion of unity . . . I am amazed by the terrifying stupidity of the illusion of unity, and by its incomprehensible force.[39]

Nomadism refers to a kind of critical consciousness which subverts set conventions. It requires what Braidotti calls the "philosophy of what-if," which is much like Ricoeur's "seeing-as." Both "what ifing" and "seeing as" are re-associative practices connected to the ontological. One does not simply practice associations, one *is in* a re-associative state. An example of this type of performative nomadism is Laurie Anderson's performance art? Anderson represents a constant flow of experience, a continuum of different levels of experience, in order to reveal conceptual paradoxes. ("It is not the bullet that kills you but the hole.") Events, experiences, and concepts are reversed or in some way re-associated. "What-ifing" both requires and engenders alternative forms of agency; "the practice of "as-if" is a technique of strategic re-location and it can be utilized to "rescue what we need of the past in order to trace paths of transformation of our lives here and now."[40]

Braidotti finds that there is no adequate conceptual representation of a state she experiences intimately as her own way of being:

> a nomad's identity is a map of where s/he has already been; s/he can always reconstruct it a posteriori, as a set of steps in an itinerary. But there is no triumphant *cogito* supervising the contingency of the self... the nomad's identity is an inventory of traces.[41]

Nomadic practice involves several elements. First, there is extensive borrowing from various disciplines; it is inter-disciplinary. Second, it involves deliberately using concepts out of context, derouted from their initial purpose, destabilizing commonsensical meanings and deconstructing established norms of association. Third, the stand point of the nomad in-between languages constitutes a unique and privileged perspective for both deconstruction and re-association. Fourth, nomadic practice involves mixing voices, combining a mixture of dry theoretical language with the lyrical or poetic. And fifth, it appropriates Spivak's technique of "the principle of quotations citations,"[42] which is a practice in the "dethroning of the 'transcendental narcissism' of the philosophizing 'I.'"[43] In other words, letting the voices of others into one's text is a way of "actualizing the noncentrality of the 'I' in the project of thinking," and recognizing theorizing as a collective project. Spivak's own critical work does not attempt to explain the words of others. She simply lets them speak, at length, for themselves. In this way she does not appropriate their words, rather, she joins in with what they are claiming thereby creating a sense of solidarity of subject position.

In Western thought the classical notion of the subject is defined in terms of sameness, that is, it remains one and the same in all its variety of qualifications and attributes, but Braidotti wants to redefine consciousness in terms of multiple layers of experience which do not privilege rationality as the organizing principle. She wants to pull apart the modern presumption of a connection between the subject and consciousness, the notion of the subject *as* consciousness, and looks instead to the unconscious as a creative field. The "key" to understanding multiple identity is unconscious process.

While some feminist theorists have argued that the postmodern denial of unified identity and the critique of metanarratives has undermined women's political agency,[44] Braidotti argues that political agency "has to do with the capacity to expose the illusion of ontological foundations." In fact what is political is the "active quest for possibilities of resistance to hegemonic formations."[45] Braidotti agrees with Butler when Butler says, "the task is to interrogate what the theoretical move that establishes foundations authorizes, and what precisely it excludes or forecloses."[46]

Like Ricoeur, the four theorists I have examined above (Spivak, Butler, Kumar, and Braidotti) all recognize the artificial nature of the "unity" of the subject. That is to say that each of these theorists recognizes that the internal coherence of the subject is a socially instituted ideal rather than a natural phenomenon. But these four theorists deconstruct the regulatory practices, the legitimizing and exclusionary practices for identity formation that Ricoeurean structural criteria represent. All four theorists are interested in critical strategies and sources of subversion for resisting assimilation into traditional ways of representing the self. Beginning with the assumption of the self as a discursive formation, they each contribute techniques for representational subversion. I will show, in the chapters that follow, that these techniques are put into practice in *Fault Lines*.

Meena Alexander's memoir, *Fault Lines*, is an example of a practice in self-narrative which engages and unlearns the tradition of unified narrative. It subverts discursive and identity-forming practices by engaging in precisely the types of de-regulatory practices that Spivak, Butler, Kumar, and Braidotti are interested in. Further, Alexander's memoir not only illustrates the subversive language play that these four feminists theorize, this memoir destabilizes traditional identity constructions by exposing their homogenizing functions. *Fault Lines* represents a critical consciousness in a re-associative state of being.

Part II : *Fault Lines*

As an introduction to her memoir, Meena Alexander enumerates the difficulties for a woman like herself to tell her life story. They include: 1. the problems of consistent identity associated with dislocation, 2. the difficulty of writing in one's own voice when one has not one, but multiple voices resulting from experiences in a multitude of places and in various languages, and, 3. the difficulty of writing as a woman when one's cultural tradition associates women and language with shame.

One of the richest sections of the memoir, "Stone-Eating Girl," focuses on a particular incident that epitomizes her problem. Once, when the narrator was a child, her reaction to her own sense of dislocation and resulting "unfixed identity," was to swallow a stone. Travel, existing in between places, was a large part of her childhood experience and the feeling of having no identity when dislocated from place demonstrates the need for the corporeal in a theory of identity. She wondered, "What was I when I was not quite in one place, nor another, just in mid-stream? Was I unfit to see?" And then she picked up a round pebble and swallowed it along with the confusion that the previous question had caused: "Swallowing that stone gave me a sense of comfort, of power even . . . I felt I was a child who could sustain something hard and solid inside her."[47] The very next day, she saw a young girl in the marketplace sitting under a tree swallowing stones. This image will become a central image for Alexander—it is both an image of shamelessness and of strength.

She, the stone-eater, was sitting under a tree with a mouth full of stones. Making an exhibit of herself in this way, she was considered shameless: "The Malayalam word for shameless, *Perachathe*, as in shameless-mad, as in mad-dog, bitch bitches being rabid, rabid dogs being known as bitches."[48] It seemed to her that the price for being *Perachathe*—shameless—was to have one's mouth filled with stones, "choosing stones, filling one's mouth with them, ejecting them through the miraculous gut we call the imagination."[49] And three decades after seeing the stone-eating girl, she is still a type of heroine:

> She taught herself whatever skills she had, learnt to use them in her own way, and set herself up as her own authority so that in her unmitigated gluttony . . . she became a female icon, creator of a stem discipline, perfecter of an art.[50]

Alexander goes on to narrate her own pre-occupation with, and talent in, developing the art of stone-eating. Her problem is like St. Augustine's experiential discordance but her problem is more acute due to dislocation. Her *solution* is different from the one Ricoeur proposes because, in part, her solution to consistent identity in the face of flux is found by grounding the body in *place* while Ricoeur's solution has to do with *intention* to remain the same in the face of change.

A conflicting image that haunts Alexander's childhood is one that goes hand in hand with the image of the stone-eating girl. The image is that of women jumping into wells, killing themselves out of shame. Something tells her that she comes from a long line of well-jumped woman.[51] She eventually comes to the realization that the kind of strength displayed by the stone-eating girl requires the same type of silence that a well-jumper epitomizes, even though the latter is shameful and the prior is shameless. It is the strength associated with silence that she had to unlearn in order to write herself "into being."

How does one with broken geography, one with fragmented experience, one who is multi-lingual and multi-cultural, tell a traditionally structured personal narrative while speaking in her own voice? She asks, "How would I map this all in a book of days? After all, my life did not fall into the narratives I had been taught to honor, tales that closed back on themselves, as a snake might, swallowing its own ending."[52] She is a woman "cracked by multiple migrations," uprooted so many times she can "connect nothing with nothing."[53] And she says "there is a real problem for me. What part of my past can I hold onto when I enter this life? Must I dump it all?[54] Recall that in a Ricoeurean narrative, discontinuities are either homogenized or they are simply omitted.

Alexander is not unaware of the traditional requirements of narrative unity; the problem is that her experience is too radically fractured to fit into this traditional structure. It is clear that this memoir is an attempt to consciously, narratively, structure an alternative identity. This is not simply a description or a recounting or recalling; this is a creative act. Alexander narrates herself into being, or, in the Ricoeurean sense, she creates herself as she performs her story. But she does something further; in a very un-Ricoeurean move; she plays with the very structure of unity and wholeness of traditional narrative. Plotting is still an act of bestowing meaning. But the meaning of experience has to do with the context of those experiences and contexts are not only temporal; they are also spatial. The temporal orientation of traditional plot structure does not fully determine the meaning of Alexander's experiences. In other words, the meaning of experience is not determined by where it fits into an Aristotelian narrative. This is not the homogenized ordered narrative of a unified subject, and the meaning that is determined by her narrative structure is not stable. Events and experiences are arranged and re-arranged in order to multiply the possibilities for meaning. This is a narrative which represents a subject in a re-associative state and her narrative structure reflects that state.

For Ricoeur particular experiences have meaning to the extent to which they contribute to the plot. And because the master plot structure is an Aristotelian-based one, the meaning of experiences becomes determined by the manner in which it contributes to the assumed structure of the whole story. For example, in the personal memoir which is the focus of this chapter, the narrator describes the feeling of having lived many lives, which together would be incohesive, incommensurable. She wonders where she should begin a narrative; at the beginning of which life? This narrator has experienced many beginnings, but Ricoeurean structure would either omit these experiences or would have what she experiences as "beginnings" assimilated as another part of the narrative. These experiences would be assigned different meaning in a Ricoeurean narrative structure. There can be only one beginning, and beginning material cannot just pop up anywhere in Aristotelian plot structure. But the narrative structure Alexander employs is determined by something other than the internalized form of the traditional plot. It is determined by the ontological state Ricoeur calls "being-as" and what Rosi Braidotti calls "as-ifing." More about this later.

Early in her memoir Alexander explains not only the inadequacy of traditional Western narrative structure for her narrative identity, but also the fact that her own tradition provides only partial assistance. The traditional Indian sense of identity is completely bound up with family, with social place, with ancestral site. But this narrator has been physically dislocated from ancestral site, family, and social place, so that this sense of identity is not completely accessible to her. She is forced to look beyond either tradition and yet neither tradition is completely left behind.

Tradition enters in even if only as a target of attack. Radical dislocation has forced Alexander to "fabricate" links to place, to "weave tales" between traditions. An example of this type of imaginative fabrication is that while the narrator does not accept the female role her mother would impose, she does not completely reject it either. She uses each of the conflicting narratives as part of her narrative material because these conflicts are part of what makes her who she is. This is what Spivak refers to as new narrations of older scripts.[55] In this way history is not denied; it is imbued with various alternative meanings. It is in this sense that Alexander exercises creative option:

> In my dreams, I am haunted by thought of a homeland I will never find. So I have tuned my lines to a different aesthetic, one that I build up out of all the stuff around me, improvising as I go along.[56]

Radical dislocation, the lack of any ancestral figure with whom she can identify, and her unashamed use and manipulation of language, make the traditional Indian sense of self inaccessible to her.

The narrator says that she has always experienced tension between multiple worlds, multiple languages, multiple selves. But through the manipulation of traditional paradigms she is able to structure a story which can encompass the conflict. And again, the notion of place plays an important role,

> For me, poems made real places. They had to, my life was so torn up into bits and pieces of the actual that I depended on the poems, irruptions of the imaginary to make an internal history for me.[57]

In a chapter called "Language and Shame," Alexander echos what the subjects of Kumar's studies have shown, and what Braidotti and Spivak both suggest, that to move between cultures and languages and traditions with incommensurable world views allows for an extended sense of agency. Alexander makes a connection between how she came to language and what it means to be dislocated.[58] She speaks English, Hindi, Arabic, French, and Malayalam, but her first poems were written in French as she does not read or write Malayalam, her mother tongue. She feels that this inability has allowed her to maintain an immediacy to sound, which in turn enabled her to partially dissolve the canonical burden of British English. A form of linguistic decolonization, which had to do with her sense of femaleness, took place:

> I set the hierarchies, the scripts aside, and let the treasured orality flow over me. After all, that is how Malayalam had first come to me: in chants, in spoken voices that held a community together.[59]

Narrative structure required by one with experiences such as hers must be more inclusive than Ricoeur's. Alexander needs a narrative structure that accommodates anomalous discontinuous cross-cultural experiences without making these experiences *the* story. Ricoeur would refigure a life like Alexander's by telling it in such a way that change and discontinuity is narrated as the constant, that is, change would *be* the continuity. But Alexander insists that she is more than a collection of fault lines, more than *just* the ruptures in her experience, more than an entity between two locations. Alexander wants to tell her personal narrative in a way that includes the parts of her past, the parts of her experiences, the parts of her way of being that *she* has determined the meaning of. She needs a narrative structure that will accommodate the meaning she has assigned her experiences rather than a structure which will determine the meaning of her experiences. Her narrative still makes sense of things retrospectively but it also encompasses multiple and even conflicting voices: "I needed others, multiple voices, a plot however simple, a form from which history could not be torn out."[60] Only structural expansion, which I delineate in the following chapter, can accommodate the demands of competing stories and conflicting voices.

Alexander uses a metaphor of hand stitching to describe the traditional model of self narration:

> fix it tightly in place . . . make the stitches as evenly as possible, tight and hard, so the silk could blend into the fabric and the frayed bit turn invisible in the well groomed sheen of the skirt or blouse.[61]

And she knows that she is living in worlds in which this kind of stitching will not do: "I needed my stitching to be like my writing to show its seams, its baste lines, its labor." The identities Alexander experiences intimately as her own are made up from the experiences in between the "events" of traditional narrative. If she told her narrative in the traditional structure the experiences in the fault lines would either be precluded from the narrative or they would be distorted. Alexander practices what Spivak insists upon—that the writer should always explicitly state her subject position. By clearly delineating one's subject position, one implies the non-universality of the theory or claim or observation. This practice demonstrates that a claim or representation cannot be separated from the cultural/linguistic construction of the subject making the claim or representation. In this sense the theory or claim or representation is not the product of unique autonomous "I," but rather a product of a point of intersection between maze of cultural and linguistic influences. Alexander offers a figuration of subjectivity that has no pretense to universality, transglobalism, or a-historical status. And the representation of her subjectivity does not aim at fluidity or unity or wholeness. Instead, Alexander's self-representation not only reflects the fabricated nature of her narrative identity, but also implicit in this aesthetic choice is a critique of any attempt to represent a self as whole and unified. Her narrative construction does not build itself upon received paradigms. It is improvised and temporary and its structure reflects its status as a work-in-progress,

> There is no ideal poise in its construction, just the basting together of bits. Sometimes bits burst open, split apart, and one does not quite know how to go on. Still, how to construct a provisional self to live by how to make up memory?[62]

She sees herself as a fissured thing, "homeless, shelterless, with no fixed place to belong, and a babbler of multiple tongues." Alexander calls herself a "nowhere creature," a body crossed by fault lines.[63] Her narrative must necessarily "invoke a chaos," which reflects her experience. Not simple *mimesis,* but re-figured chaos. Narratively, one can "map out a provisional self." But traditional whole/unified narrative structure is inadequate for the narration of her life story. She insists that:

> talk of wholeness . . . really doesn't make sense, or if it does only as a trope for the mind that casts back where-ever it is and whenever for a beforeness that is integral in precisely the ways that only a past can be.[64]

In this chapter I have attempted to show precisely how the structural requirements of Narrative Identity Theory turn out to demand more from some forms of life than others. The more discontinuous experience is, the more difficult the narrative task. Physical dislocation, cultural incompatibility, and the struggle for narrative voice, are structurally challenging experiences and in Ricoeur's system they heighten the distortion requirement. In Ricoeurean terms, the more discordant the experience, the more violent the interpretation.

Chapter III

Comparative Analysis

The previous chapter described the problems associated with narrating within traditional structure. This chapter will provide a comparative analysis of *Fault Lines* and Ricoeurean aesthetic criteria in order to show that *Fault Lines* does not meet Ricoeurean structural requirements of unified/whole plot structure nor that of concordance. This project will require three steps. First I will remind the reader of Ricoeurean structural criteria. Then these criteria will be applied to the narrative structure of *Fault Lines* in order to provide a type of conceptual overlay so the reader can see precisely where and how these structures differ. It will be left for the following chapters to provide the third step by arguing that while *Fault Lines* does not meet Ricoeurean criteria it nonetheless provides experience with structure, and it *functions* in the manner essential to any conception of narrative identity—identity is created in the process of telling its story.

The first consequence of an alternative structure results from the way Alexander makes sense of time. This alternative structure narratively "configures" human temporal experience, but it does so differently than Ricoeur would have it. The second consequence of Alexander's alternative plot structure is that personal identity is predicated upon features of experience entirely different from those required for Ricoeurean narrative identity. Of the two primary consequences of Alexander's plot, the second one is the one that interests me in this chapter

Part I: Traditional Structure

Recall that the project of *Time and Narrative* was to provide a solution to Augustine's problem with time via an extension of Aristotelian poetic theory. In Aristotle's concept of emplotment (*muthos*) Ricoeur finds the answer to Augustine's problem with the existential burden of discordance. But the problem with Aristotle, according to Ricoeur, is that he confuses *mimesis* with *muthos*—imitation with emplotment. Moreover, there is no mention in Aristotle of the connection between poetic activity and temporal experience. It is here that Ricoeur wants to contribute.

A plot meets the Ricoeurean criteria of *wholeness/completeness* and *unity* if it has a beginning, middle, and end, each necessitated by what precedes or follows it. Aristotle explains these criteria as follows:

> Now a whole is that which has a beginning, middle, and end. A beginning is that which is not itself necessarily after any-thing else, and which has naturally something else after it; an end is that which is naturally after something itself, either as its necessary or usual consequent, and with nothing else after it; and a middle, that is by nature after one thing and has also another after it. A well constructed plot, therefore, cannot either begin or end at any point one likes; beginning and end in it must be of the forms just described.[1]

The beginning, middle, and end are not features of experience, they are the effects of an ordering plot. And *mimesis* should be understood, not as imitation of some pre-existing reality, but rather as creative imitation. This kind of *mimesis* is not Platonic imitation in the sense of re-duplication of a particular. Aristotelian *mimesis* implies poetic re-figuration. As Ricoeur sees it, "we have to understand something completely contrary to a copy of some preexisting reality and speak instead of creative imitation . . . Artisans who work with words produce not things but quasi-things; they invent the as-if."[2]

While Ricoeur wants to preserve the Aristotelian sense of *muthos* and *mimesis* as operations, as activities,[3] he wants to "broaden, radicalize, and enrich" the Aristotelian notion of *muthos*, emplotment, and he also wants to contribute to the notion of time handed down by Augustine. He does this by exploring the resources of narrative configuration. On the formal level, plot is defined as *concordance*: "an integrating dynamism that draws a unified and complete story from a variety of incidents . . . transforms this variety into a unified and complete story."[4] Plot is called "a new congruence in the organization of events."[5] It "grasps together and integrates into one whole and complete story multiple and scattered events, thereby schematizing the intelligible signification attached to the narrative taken as a whole."[6] Then the Aristotelian notion of muthos is extended, thereby creating,

> rule governed transformations worthy of being called plots so long as we can discern temporal wholes bringing about a synthesis of the heterogeneous.[7]

The configuring act of emplotment is a "judicative act, involving grasping together"[8] which requires a type of reflective judgment. This is reflective judgment in the Kantian aesthetic sense. In narrative terms, reflective judgment involves retrospective reflection over lots of experiences in search of a unifying theme. And there must be one dominant narrative voice, a Master-voice. There is no room for what Ricoeur calls the "polyphonic."[9]

In the preface to the first volume of *Time and Narrative* we told that metaphor and narrative are alike in the sense that they are both phenomena of semantic innovation; they involve linguistic synthesis of the heterogeneous. The semantic innovation of metaphor lies in its production of new semantic pertinence through displacement. The semantic innovation of narrative lies in its creating a synthesis, in the form of a plot. "By means of plot, goals, causes, and chance are brought together within the temporal unity of the whole and complete action."[10]

Unity, wholeness, and concordance are all essential features of Ricoeurean plot. The imitation of action ordered in this way will have the effect of re-constituting our subjective experience of time: "I see in the plots we invent the privileged means by which we re-configure our confused, unformed, and at the limit mute temporal existence."

So, *unity/wholeness* and *concordance* are the structural criteria, and the *re-constitution of temporal experience* is one of the effects of Ricoeurean plot. The other effect is the *synthesis of experience.* Ricoeur's normative ideal of narrative unity and the resulting identity of the self marginalizes less prototypical forms of narrative, exemplified by *Fault Lines,* as less coherent and, by implication of his emphasis on *ipse,* less ethical.

Part II: Alternative Structures

Meena Alexander engages traditional narrative construction in the Aristotelian model but ultimately she deconstructs it and constructs a self based on a poetic re-construction of intense past experiences. Her narrative is not unified/whole and does not function as a synthesizer of experience. It does not have a single beginning, but multiple beginnings. And it remains open-ended. Not only does it leave room for re-figuration on the part of the reader, the text doesn't end itself. It does not gather similar experiences and artificially string them together.

Any potential for textual linearity is interrupted by poems or the recreation of remembered feeling. Poetry surfaces at crucial moments—moments of transfer, fissure, disjuncture. The many starts of *Fault Lines* reflect the effort to make sense of experienced time with regard to measured time. The narrative denies a beginning by giving several false starts. It gives instead a plethora of traditional "beginnings" so that there is not one but many beginnings. The text refuses to give us a grounding initial event, a beginning episode. There are intense moments followed by rupture and breaks. For example, Alexander's story about being denied tenure is immediately followed the narration of a childhood memory. The reader is taken from an American university to the cashew and mango trees of India. The reader enters the narrative in present tense, *in media res,* setting the stage for the narrator's reflections on the past. This is a common enough device. But then the reader is taken back, not to the birth of the narrator and main character, but to the multiple births of her grandparents and parents. This differs from the technique of beginning *in media res* in traditional structure because it goes not begin *in media res* and then go back to the beginning. There is not one particular beginning to bo back to. There are multiple beginnings, multiple births. The representation of multiple beginnings is not an attempt to contextualize her narrative within a larger structure in the traditional manner; rather, she includes these multiple births as a part of her own narrative. This narrator feels that she has been born in many times in many places. Certain aspects of traditional Indian identity are imported as Alexander emphasizes the location of her grandparents' and parents' births as well as the "pattern of naming." The introductory pages of *Fault Lines*, pages that traditionally tell the beginning of the story, tell of place. Alexander's narrative begins with her significant place—the ancestral home.

The first half of the second chapter is as close as this narrative comes to any resemblance of traditional beginning. But even then,

> Multiple birth dates ripple, sing inside me, as if a long stretch of silk were passing through my fingers. I think of the lives I have known for forty years, the lives unknown, the shining geographies that feed into the substance of any possible story I might have. As I make up a katha, a story of my life, the lives before me, around me, weave into a net without which I would drop ceaselessly. They keep me within range of difficult truths, the exhilarating dangers of memory.[11]

Then an image of the narrator's grandmother is associated with contemporary life in New York. But abruptly, in the middle of the second chapter, the narrative begins again: "My earliest years flow back: skin, cotton, wall, mattress, and quilt."[12] The story of the early years is full of sensual images. A second beginning[13] precedes a break—referred to as a "fault line." This interruption is immediately followed by an abrupt return to the present[14] which is followed by a jump to the near distant past which sounds like the beginning of another story, "lying on the bed all alone one summer afternoon."[15] This image begins a memory/dream concerned with place and time. And this memory/dream is followed by yet another narrative beginning, the story of the narrator's birth.

Now, Ricoeur would understand all of these jumps and breaks relative to a larger narrative that is being constructed as the narrator encounters each of these incidents. Ricoeur himself admits that the tacitly assumed narrative structure will determine the way we understand breaks and ruptures in continuous experience. The problem for Alexander is that these types of experiential ruptures are a primary part of her life experience and to assimilate them in a Ricoeurean narrative would be to silence precisely the types of experiences that Alexander claims are important to her own sense of self. But Aristotelian poetic structure is tacitly assumed, how is

Alexander able to avoid it? If the way we understand experience is pre-figures, how can we experience our experience any other way?

The answer to this question lies in the very aspect of Alexander's narrative that makes it less prototypical: she exists in the fault lines between the conceptual systems of several cultures. Alexander is a nomad. She is a linguistic polyglot, in the Braidottian sense, who travels between worlds, languages, and conceptual schemes. This form of existence enables a form of postcolonial narrative agency that undermines traditional associations, regulatory discursive practices, and structures of self-representation.

Alexander is aware of how traditional narratives begin but, for her, "multiple birth dates ripple." Her observations shift from childhood memories to images of contemporary New York to dreams in adolescence to "imaged" role models. Then about one-fourth of the way through the memoir the story of her birth is re-created:

> I was born out of my mother, and out of her mother before her, and her mother, and her mother, and hers. Womb blood and womb tissue flowing, gleaming, no stopping. I was born in Allahabad, in Uttar Pradesh, in the plains of northern India the great city of God, where two rivers meet, the Ganga and the Jamuna.[16]

This passage works to contextualize her narrative; it is a type of narrative embedding, but this passage does more. By appearing one-fourth of the way through the memoir, it disrupts potential linearity. By including ancestral place it incorporates part of a traditional Indian sense of self. Alexander goes on to re-create a story of her arrival at home, as a new born, complete with details like a muslin covered mattress and cheeks puffed from sucking. Recollection here is an imaginative act. The past is re-created by re-association of events and experiences. it is not that Alexander does not structure her experiences; she does. But in contrast with Ricoeur, Alexander does not synthesize hererogeneous experience. Instead, she opens up the field of association and loosens the grip of traditional chronological linking. She says, "The literal is always discrepant, a sharp otherness to what the imagination conjures up as it blends time."[17] Time, for Alexander, is not fluid or whole. Her past is full of ghosts, and the past that haunts her is often an imaginary past. This narrative moves ahead by moving back—back to important events, recollections, dreams. Ordinary daily events, like riding the subway, or cooking, are combined with ideas and thoughts and dreams so that there is a sense of internal life mixed with experience of the external world.

The story of her birth is a good example of the way in which three consistent themes of the memoir are presented—dislocation, imagination, and identity. This birth story is an imaginatively re-created beginning; it is an example of an alternative to Ricoeur's "figuration" involving organizational unity. This "figuration," in the Braidottian sense, is a re-created image (in this case birth story as the traditional beginning) which functions to imaginatively structure (in the sense of give meaning to) an event, a past, in a distant place. Alexander's birth story does not serve as the "beginning" of the narrative. In fact, the ambiguities surrounding her birth contribute to the sense of a displaced "beginning" episode. There is not one but many birth stories. The purpose of these stories is not to "ground" the narrative in a beginning episode nor is it the purpose of the birth story to introduce a "middle." The birth stories function to represent a type of experience that this narrator feels more intimately than a birth she can't remember or details that don't seem to matter. Alexander's multiple birth stories represent what she experiences as being born many times in many places.

Alexander repeats several times that there is uncertainty concerning the time of her physical birth. "I do not know who cut my umbilical cord. Or how it was cut. Did he use scissors? Perhaps it was a harassed doctor. Perhaps a nurse held me, all slippery and mussed, my head a purplish cone with the pressure of entry."[18] No one will tell her the exact time of her birth, but as regards place, the tone is much more certain,

> Though I was born there, Allahabad is not my home. It is far from Tiruvella, about a thousand miles due north. Nadu is the Malayalam word for home, for homeland. Tiruvella, where my mother's home, Kuruchiethu House, stands, and Kozencheri, where appa's home, Kannadical House, stands, together compose my nadu, the dark soil of self. I was taught that what I am is bound up always with a particular ancestral site.[19]

Lt me pause for a moment to summarize. Alexander's memoir has multiple beginnings recurring repeatedly throughout the narrative. Even the final chapter contains a re-telling of a beginning. These beginnings do not lead to a middle. There is no middle that leads to a resolved ending. There is a girlhood in the narrative but girlhood is not represented as an intermediate stage between childhood and adulthood. It does not function to connect the two. It is not in the "middle" of the narrative. What would be the material of the middle of the traditional narrative is scattered from start to finish. Then at the beginning of the end of the memoir, the narrator tells the story of her mother's marriage, thereby presenting both an image of "the feminine form of transportation" (moving to the husband's ancestral home), and the ritual of what, in India, is typically considered the "beginning" of a woman's life. This is not the first time, or the second or third time, that this particular Katha (life story) has been told. It has been re-told and re-constructed several times in the course of the memoir. The point is *not* that Alexander cannot fit these multiple beginnings into a coherent and unified narrative. The point is that to do so would be to tell a colonized narrative. It would preclude some of Alexander's experience and distort the rest of it. Ricoeur's narrative criteria exclude most of the experiences that Alexander values, but it also imposes a narrative structure that obscures and even denies ways in which the stories of non-dominant groups, nomads, border dwellers, differ from dominant groups. Above I have shown, for example, what Alexander experiences as multiple beginnings would be understood or configured differently, if they were included at all, in a Ricoeurean narrative. Allowing an inherited structure to determine the meaning one assigns to one's experience is a practice in what Spivak terms trained self-effacement. Alexander wants to exercise her narrative agency in a different way.

The telling and re-telling of multiple imagined beginnings is not an attempt to ground herself in a narrative beginning, nor to serve as a signal to the reader that the narrative has begun; rather this is an experiment with different and various "modes of being toward the past." It is an attempt to account for the effect of past experiences on present identity. The question is, to what degree, and in what manner, if at all, can the past account for who one is? This is the question continually re-worked in the narration of beginnings. One might expect that this narrative would have multiple endings but in fact it has no ending, that is, it remains open-ended, "there is no ideal poise in its construction, just the basting together of bits. Sometimes bits burst open, split apart."[20] This alternative to traditional modes of self-representation is not just a method of subverting conventions of representing unified subjectivity; it is a method of creating new forms of decentered subjectivity.

Fault Lines is not monological; it allows for multiple narrative voices. For example, the narrator tells of an imaginary conversation she had with an imaginary friend. The conversation is her way of recalling the past, and of making sense of the disjuncture and abrupt interruptions of experience by telling herself a story. In this inner dialogue between herself and an imagined other she tells her story as she would tell it to another. But the story isn't designed to link events together temporally; her experiences are too radically ruptured. Alexander does not make sense of, or give meaning to, events by linking them together chronologically. Rather, from her re-associative mode of being, past events, dreams, imagined figurations, images, other modes of being, are linked together. This is imaginative linking, metaphorical association. This association is not completely free-floating; anything is not just linked with anything else. But this re-association *is* less restricted than Ricoeur's. For example, particular experiences and events may be narrated together because the meaning she assigns them are associated, not because they occurred at the same time. So, this "birth" may be like that "birth" even if they occur twenty years apart. Or experiences in the past may be associated with poetic reconstructions of past experiences. The logic of this linking is poetic association. Stylistically the narrative devices match the abrupt change brought by air travel, the failure of memory, and the grace of imagination. Events are not ordered sequentially, and memories, dreams, a "made up past," imagined speech, all roll in together. The "mapping of the provisional self" occurs in bits of this and pieces of that assembled according to no conventional rules. Experience is recalled and fabricated and dismantled and reassembled in the interest of constructing a provisional self.

So instead of temporal structuring, this narrative linking is more free-floating. Readers are taken from one place to another and from distant past to the present, then back to the near past, and on and on. This organization is open to change as are the meanings assigned to experience. Meanings will be re-assigned and past events will be re-organized. It is in this sense that agent-determined meaning determines the structure of the narrative rather than narrative structure determining meaning, as Ricoeur would have it. Ricoeur insists that, "We do not ask what the hero did between two events that would have been separated in his life."[21] But Alexander narratively creates essential elements of identity by including some of the experiences that traditional narrative skips or represses, such as the experiences in between "events" and places. Ricoeurean *mimesis* of action does not concern itself with what the hero did between episodes of action, but *Fault Lines* is full of experiences and consciousness between the "events" and "actions" that make up traditional narratives. It is full of borders, rupture, the chaos between events. For example, in describing her move from Hydrabad to New York City, te narrative material consists of neither of these two places, but the consciousness of being in-between. "My two worlds, present and past, were torn apart, and I was the fault line, the crack that marked the dislocation."[22] She refers to fault lines as "fissures in the ground . . . caused by the shifting of underground plates."[23] But it is imperative to understand that Alexander's narrative does not consist *only* of the experiences between events. She:

> wanted to become more than (a) thing that marked out the boundaries between worlds. More than a mere line in the dry earth. I wanted to give voice to my flesh, to learn to live as a woman. To do this, I had to spit out the stones that were in my mouth. I had to spit out the stones that were in my mouth. I had to become a ghost, enter my own flesh.[24]

In a section called "Crossing Boarders," Alexander links dislocation and imagination. Imagination serves an essential meaning-making function for the extremely displaced narrator. She describes the many moves over her lifetime, her utter sense of dislocation, which is epitomized by imagery of her first ocean voyage across the Arabian Sea,

> That first ocean voyage obsesses me. I think of it as a figuration of death. Losing sense, being blotted out, thrown irretrievably across a border. But it also provoked the imagery. I am forced to fabricate, trust to the maquillage of words, weave tales.[25]

The second chapter is closed with the image of crossing borders, travel, exile. It is the recurring image of her first ocean voyage: "my days changed utterly and I became a child of a different type. My life shattered into little bits and pieces."[26]

Part III: Analysis

Several aspects of Ricoeur's narrative theory are troubling; for example, Ricoeur's vision of catharsis, and what he calls "the question of confidence" of the reader, and what seems to be simply an aesthetic distaste for alternative narrative structures. But I have not argued these points. Nor will I argue for the precise opposite of what Ricoeur clings to—formlessness. What I am interested in is alternative narrative structures—plots which provide reflection with a way to assign value to discordant experience without synthesizing it.

Ricoeur's Aristotelian solution to Augustine's time problem is too conservative, and what is required is a more encompassing conception of plot. Meena Alexander's narrative treatment of space, place, and time provides an example of an alternative structure and resulting identity.

It has been my thesis that Ricoeur's notion of the identity of the subject as narratively produced is on the right track but his aesthetic preference for wholeness is problematic. While he claims to denounce any notion of meta-narrative, Ricoeur's conception of narrative is completely paradigmatic. There is no discernible difference between what he calls "paradigms" ("paradigms . . . furnish the rules for a subsequent experimentation"[27]) and what is renounced as meta-narrative, ("Rule-governed deformation constitutes the axis around which the various changes of paradigm through application are arranged").[28] Remember that for Ricoeur, narrative is still the "paradigm of order" wherein "configuration wins out over the episodic form, concordance overcomes discordance."[29] He insists on narrative wholeness, resolved endings, and he claims that polyphonic novels (stories with multiple narrative voices) are non-art. Although Ricoeur announces his alliance with the postmodern position against meta-narrative, ("The leaving behind of Hegeleanism signifies renouncing the attempt to decipher the supreme plot"), he seems to be afraid of where the critique of meta-narrative leaves narrative. His fear is that without the imposition of his particular brand of order, story-telling will have no place: "I shall ask whether this contestation (of the formal paradigm of discordant concordance) . . . does not signify the death of the narrative form itself."[30] He fears, "Nothing . . . excludes the possibility that the metamorphosis of the plot will encounter somewhere a boundary beyond which we can no longer recognize the formal principle of temporal configuration that makes a story a whole and complete story. And yet . . . and yet."[31] And yet Ricoeur has hope. His hope is that new narrative forms will be created for which we have no names yet, which will metamorphize the narrative function without allowing it to die. It is precisely this hope that *Fault Lines* exemplifies.

Meena Alexander possesses a type of narrative identity she calls "the poetic self" which is structured upon her "kathas" (life stories), but the structure of her narrative does not function to synthesize or unify her experience or her reflections upon her experience with a "sedimented" "paradigm." Rather, she is involved in the ever-changing process of reflectively assigning and re-assigning meaning and value to experience. This memoir retains the best features of narrative identity without its central feature—discordant concordance. The narrative activity is more imaginative than what is required by discordant/concordance because traditional associations are deconstructed and creative "Play" establishes new, provisional and temporary, associations.

Alexander's plot does not represent a temporal whole which brings about a synthesis of heterogeneous experience as Ricoeur would have it, nor is it singularly *mimesis* of action. And, contrary to another Ricoeurean criterion, *Fault Lines* is polyphonic. But Alexander's narrative does not do what Ricoeur fears is *mimesis* at its worst—imitate the chaos of reality. This narrative act *is* an act of structuring accomplished through assigning meaning to experience retrospectively. But this structure does not meet Ricoeur's requirements for narrative. Alexander plays with the organization to explore new ways to give experience meaning, more precisely, to attach new meaning to experience. In this way Alexander extends Ricoeur's idea that by narrating one appropriates. To narrate is to exert agency, even over the involuntary, by assigning it meaning in relation to other events and experiences in our lives. One extends narrative agency by extending the field of association. Experiences are not necessarily grouped together with other similar experiences; often times they are associated with very heterogeneous experiences, with dreams, poems, utopian visions.

According to Ricoeur, the sufficient conditions for narrative are: 1. temporal orientation, 2. unity, 3. wholeness, 4. univocity, 5. discordant/concordance, and 6. *mimesis* of *action* rather than of consciousness, or character. My claim is that a sufficient condition for "narrative" is (non-permanent) representation of agent-determined meaning. This does not mean that a subject "makes up" meaning, because the subject's imagination is limited to re-association. It is thereby imperative that this associative process be liberalized.

Although Alexander's plot does not function as concordant discordance in the Ricoeurean sense, her narrative has the same type of relationship to personal identity that contemporary theories of narrative identity elucidate. This memoir plays games with time but does not meet requirements for unity and wholeness. Nor does *Fault Lines* replicate the chaos of the narrator's lived experience; that chaos is communicated but not imitate. This memoir is Alexander's attempt to reflect upon what her past has to do with the selves she is now. It is both an attempt to provide past experiences with meaning derived from the present and an attempt to gather for the present self-useful material for identity construction from the past. *Fault Lines* represents a creative attempt to re-organize the narration of past experience as part of a method of identity construction. Alexander is always aware of her writing as a method of self-creation: "I think I have to write myself into being . . . to evade the names they have given me."[32]

While there is action in the memoir (the literal crossing of borders, passages, voyages, transit) the weight of the memoir involves types of "figurations" of consciousness which require a different type of configuring act. Alexander's memoir is neither simple imitation nor a method for ordering discordant experience; it is an imaginative rendering of agent-assigned meaning to past and present experience. In four respects Alexander's memoir fails Ricoeur's test for narrative art because her memoir favors, 1. creative representation over concordant discordance, 2. representation of consciousness over imitation of action, 3. the inclusion of multiple voices, and 4. a non-unified plot structure. But despite its being an aesthetic failure on Ricoeurean grounds, *Fault Lines* achieves the central task of narrative according to my theory of narrative subjectivity: it provides experience with provisional and contingent meaning. *Fault Lines* does not replicate discordant experience and yet "vivid multiplicity prevails." Experience is ordered, bestowed with meaning, and then re-ordered and given a different meaning. The re-ordering, re-telling, is a continuing process.

In this chapter I have attempted to demonstrate precisely how Alexander's memoir does *not* fit the traditional unified plot structure but more importantly, and consequently, Alexander's narrative does not function as concordance. Her narrative retains the most interesting features for narrative identity theory without the traditional structure. Her structure does not silence anomalous experience. Not only does Alexander create an Internarrative Identity based on rupture rather than unity. This is an alternative "figuration" with a sense of identity related to contingency rather than consistency.

Ricoeur asks, "What is the critical threshold beyond which the most extreme deviations from this style of traditionality force upon us the hypothesis not only of a schism in relation to the narrative tradition but the death of the narrative function itself?"[33] What I have proposed in this chapter is that Alexander's memoir is an example of a narrative which *does* represent a schism in relation to the narrative tradition Ricoeur represents, but it *does not* imply the death of the narrative function; in fact, it serves as a model of a broader and richer conception of *muthos* than Ricoeur envisions.

Chapter IV

Internarrative Identity

The previous chapter sought to establish *Fault Lines* as a challenge to Ricoeur's narrative criteria, particularly, discordant concordance and unified/whole plot structure. This chapter will explore precisely what, in the traditional model, the results of the narrator's aesthetic failure are for her identity. I will demonstrate how the narrative identity of the subject is determined as much by the structure of the narrative as by the content of the story. And I will describe how a more encompassing plot structure engenders an alternative form of subjectivity, one I call Internarrative Identity.

Ricoeur's insight, in response to the Postmodern proclamation of the death of the subject, is to distinguish between identity that is given and that which is created, sameness from selfhood, *idem* from *ipse*. His oversight, I think, is to link selfhood with consistency to an overly conservative conception of plot structure. The normative ideal of narrative unity and the resulting unified self marginalizes not only other narrative forms but other voices, other selves, other ways of being. Our understanding of agency is enriched if we take narrative control not only over the stories we tell about ourselves but also over the ways in which we tell them. I think Ricoeur is right in insisting that we make ourselves who we are by making our experiences meaningful. Events and experiences do not have meaning in themselves and meaning is not created out of nothing. Meaning is determined by association.[1] But in the Ricoeurean system meaning-making is limited by restrictive principles of association. The association is necessarily temporal. An alternatively structured narrative involves alternative associations. I propose spatial association as one alternative. Experience is still made meaningful by narrating it but in my system "narrative" is not understood as a synthesizing of experience into a unified structure but rather it is understood as manipulating and re-associating experience. The narrator extends her agency by extending her field of association across cultures, languages, and conceptual systems. For Ricoeur the association is limited by a classical Western aesthetic and for Alexander it is not. As I argued in the third chapter, Alexander's repeated dislocations make narration in the Ricoeurean model very challenging for her. On the other hand, life in the fault lines has provided this narrator, like the subjects of Kumar's studies, a unique perspective and capacity for subversion of traditional associations.

A subject who lives in more than one culture may be a part of more than one narrative. She may, like Meena Alexander, have a collection of incommensurable narratives. They are incommensurable in the sense that even though there are cross-cultural associations, she is part of different narratives in different places. Even though the narratives are incompatible they are not mutually exclusive. And narrative voice shifts from place to place so that the Internarrative is what Ricoeur objects to as "polyphonic" and does not meet the requirement of a "homophonic" or "monological" voice.

The postcolonial agency[2] of an Internarrative Subject is exercised in undermining traditional associations, identity practices, and structures of self-representation. This subject may engage in subversive identity performance, reversals of concepts, and parodies of the Master-voice. Her method is poetic re-association, cross-culturally, across languages and conceptual systems. So, meaning is still determined narratively but the meaning of an event or experience is not determined by its temporal orientation in a linear plot; the meaning of an event or experience is determined by its narrative association with other events, experiences, images, spatial orientations, and then it is re-determined in the same way over and over again. Meaning is not fixed or stable, it is constantly reworked; it is derived from this narrative play.

While Ricoeur asks, "In what sense am I the same person that I was years ago?" I am interested in a question that goes further than Ricoeur's. The question is: in what sense am I the same person I was years ago *in different places?* My answer, like Ricoeur's, is a narrative one. But Internarrative Identity is created in the process of narratively mediating conceptions of "self" and "sameness" which are richer than Ricoeur's conceptions and more appropriate for the extended form of agency that I am interested in. Ricoeur's narrative criterion of discordant/concordance, the requirement that narrative must "synthesize," or "homogenize" otherwise discordant experience, is particularly demanding for those subjects with particularly discordant experience, for example, cross-cultural experience. On Ricoeur's model, the more heterogeneous the experience, the more challenging the configurational task of the narrator.

The basic principle of narrative identity theory is that personal identity is correlative to plot, that the only sense in which a self can be identified is in relation to the stories one sees oneself as a part of. The problem with this conception is that identity is not simply emplotted, it is emplotted in a very particular type of narrative structure—one that admits only a particular type of assimilated experiential material. The experiential disjunctures which figure so prominently in multi-cultural existence Alexander's memoir are precisely the experiences that Ricoeurean plot structure excludes. Narrative Identity Theory goes further than conceptualizing identity as consistent with plot. It understands identity as correlative to the *structure* of the plot. And the structure of the plot is on this conception, Aristotelian.

The Ricoeurean conditions of plot are: temporal organization, homophony, priority of plot over character and actions over thoughts. He seems to be afraid that if narrative is not structured in the Aristotelian manner, then it will be the description, the simple imitation, of a chaotic mess of meaningless and unrelated events. But Alexander's narrative does not have to fall to his extreme. An Internarrative plot structure does all the same things that Ricoeur's plot structure does and more because association is not limited to the temporal within a whole and unified structure.

Recall the Narrative Identity diagram. There was a pole drawn on the left side and a pole on the right side. Under the pole on the right side the words "self," "*ipse*," and "promise" appear. Under the pole on the left the words "same," "*idem*," and "character" appear. Ricoeur argues that although there is a zone of overlapping, sameness and self are not only *not* the same, they are "polar opposites."[3] Identity as sameness (*idem*) is demonstrated by "character" which is exemplified by remaining the same over time. Identity as "self" (*ipse*) is demonstrated by the ethical commitment to remain the same in the face of change. An example of this type of self is evidenced in the act of keeping a promise, which serves as a "challenge to time, a denial of change," especially if change which challenges that commitment has taken place. The ethical self evidenced by the act of honoring past commitments over time is "a modality of permanence in time capable of standing as polar opposite to the permanence of character."[4] Identity is created in the continuing process of mediating between selfhood and sameness narratively.

Also recall Ricoeur's basic account of *idem*. Four types of sameness are identified: numerical identity, extreme resemblance, uninterrupted continuity, and permanence over time. It is this last type of sameness in which Ricoeur is most interested, specifically, how permanence over time is connected to selfhood. This sense of "permanence in time" means that even though aspects of a thing have changed, the overall thing remains what it was before. For example, a tool is the same tool even if all the parts have been replaced. In narrative terms, the structure is privileged over the content. To his original question, "Is there a type of permanence in time that is an answer to the question 'Who am I?'" (the formulation of the question itself being a determining gesture), Ricoeur develops the answer of narrative identity—"I" am developed in dialectic between my lasting dispositions and my commitment to honor the commitments I made in the past. On this model ethical selfhood results from intentional consistency. The honoring of past commitments takes on tremendous importance. Why is the act of keeping a promise, of honoring one's commitments, an ethical act? It is not just because it is an example of "keeping your word" or "walking your talk," it is because keeping a promise is "a denial of change, a challenge to time." Why does change or the passing of time necessitate an ethical challenge? The implication is that to be uncommitted to permanence in time is to privilege the experiences of flux, multiplicity, radical disjuncture. The imposition of a traditionally western model of structural order is posited as an ethical move.

Now, consider the manner in which a Ricoeurean narrator, responding to the request to tell about her life, could deal with the interruptions in unified experience. Her narrative could take this form: "I was born there, raised here and there, moved there, then moved again, and now I'm here." It would be a little more exciting than that; reaching "here" would be configured as the culminating event resulting from the overcoming of obstacles which developed from the original starting point (usually the narrator's birth). This is what Mark Johnson calls the "source-path-goal" structure of proto-typical narratives.[5]

Moving and traveling would be the constant, the theme, and because it is what she does in and between every culture, experience would be synthesized around this central theme—TRAVELING. Recall how adamantly Ricoeur insists that "the universal character of the formal principle of narrative configuration (is) the temporal synthesis of the heterogeneous,"[6] and that "every composition we call narrative" should be organized this way.[7] But what if, in the course of telling about herself, the narrator repeats the story of her birth five or six times? What if each time she tells about her birth, she tells it differently, so that it is a different story each time? The aesthetic assumption which becomes the foundation for Ricoeur's theory of personal identity would lead one to view such an account as a type of narrative chaos. It would be considered dissassociative[8] at best. But this narrator does not suffer from multiple personality disorder. She is *re*-associative, although this type of reassociation is not a function of a tacitly assumed structure. It is a function of a deliberately alternative structure.

The Internarrative Subject engages in what has been described as the dialectic between selfhood and sameness, but the terms are understood differently. On Ricoeur's model the words "self," "*ipse*," and "promise" appear together under one pole, and "same," "*idem*," and "character" appear together under the other pole. One's narrative identity is located somewhere mediating between these two poles. An alternative conception of self, based on our example, can be similarly schematized. Consider once again the two poles, one drawn on the left and the other on the right side of a piece of paper.

Ricoeur

ipse < ——————— Narrative Identity ——————— > *idem*

self   same

commitment   "character"

Maan

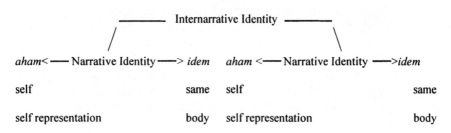

————— Internarrative Identity —————

aham<——— Narrative Identity ——> *idem*   *aham* <——— Narrative Identity ——>*idem*

self   same   self   same

self representation   body   self representation   body

As in Ricoeur's model the words "self" appears under one pole and the word "same" under the other pole. But on my alternative model, unlike Ricoeur's model, "keeping a promise" is not linked with "self" and "*ipse*." Self-consistency is not founded upon challenging changes that happen in time, but rather, by bringing a sense of the past into the present by being consciously aware of past and future in the present moment. Rather than challenging the changes brought by time, the changes challenge Alexander to re-arrange, re-create, another narrative. The new narrative will integrate past experiences and new perceptions, insights and associations as a "present" part of the narrative.[9]

Further, a diagram of my alternative conception of identity, Internarrative Identity, would replace the Latin *ipse* with the Sanskrit *aham* and the Latin *idem* with the Sanskrit *idam*. While *idem* and *idam* both denote "sameness" the type of sameness is significantly different. Ricoeur understands *idem* as undiminishingly self-same. It is the sameness of lasting dispositions. It is the type of sameness which makes an individual recognizable as the same individual over time. But the sameness of the Sanskrit *idam* si *shared* sameness. it is sameness with others. This substitution is a radical one because in my alternative model of identity sameness is not individual sameness, it is not a uniqueness that remains consistent. Instead, sameness is communal rather than individual. It has to do with commonality rather than uniqueness.[10] The consequence of this substitution is that identity is created in the process of narratively mediating the poles of self-centralization and sameness *with others* rather than mediating between the ethical commitment to deny change and defining characteristics which remain the same over time.

It has been observed that the individuation seems to be the most crucial aspect of the Western autobiographical endeavor.[11] The hero of a traditional narrative is defined by exclusionary means, by separation, by uniqueness. There is also tradition of self-construction in the West which equates agency with control and power with mastery. But in an Internarrative the emphasis is less on individuality and more on community; that is to say, there is identification through relationship rather than through individuation. The subject is a collective subject. For example in *Fault Lines* familial relations, ancestral ties, and hereditary place are extremely important to identity formation: "I was taught that what I am is bound up always with ancestral site."[12]

Still further, my alternative model has replaced Ricoeur's "character" with "body." The body represents the fourth type of permanence over time. Like Ricoeur's "tool," even though aspects of it can change, it is basically the same thing it was before the changes. "The body" replaces Ricoeur's "character" but, again, the way Ricoeur uses "character" is not the way the term is commonly understood. For him character indicates "a lasting set of dispositions" or "distinguishing characteristics" which permit the recognition of the subject as the same subject over time.

There is no ethical weight to Ricoeur's understanding of "character." Character does not involve choice: choice is found under the other pole and is associated with *ipse*. Any sense of consistent identity for Alexander is bound up with embodiment, which, like "character" for Ricoeur, is only one end of identity. The other end is narration.

Let me first explain why "the body" is a more suitable component for my conception of identity than Ricoeur's "character," then I will address self representation. Ricoeur is led to Narrative Identity Theory by his search for a sense of self that is permanent in time. But some narrators have even more of a problem; they require a sense of self that remains in various *places*. For some subjects the same temporal discordance that Augustine and Ricoeur experience is further complicated by spatial discontinuity. The only constant through temporal and spatial discontinuity is the body. One may not have an over-riding narrative which unifies her experiences. There may be multiple narratives which differ from place to place, but they are all housed in one body. The body does more work for my alternative conception than Ricoeur's idea of character does for his account of Narrative Identity, as the body is not only a locus of permanence in time because of its enduring overall structure; it is the locus of a type of permanence in time because it is the locus of memory. Past(s) and future are held together within the present, not as past remembered or future anticipated, but rather as temporally distinct moments bound together vis shared place in the present. Experiences which fracture continuous experience co-exist in memory. One need not be dependent upon narrative "wholeness" and "unity" because embodied memory holds together disparate temporal experiences. As Alexander says,

> The structures of human memory bear with them the imprint of the spatial existence of the lived body through which alone they have been generated. Thus the need to spatialize the linearity of recollected time and imbue it with the order of a *place* where the disparate temporal elements can co-exist is itself made more comprehensible. One approaches the need of St. Augustine, so full of wonder at the workings of memory, to talk about the "field" of the self.[13]

Let me explain. Precisely like Ricoeur, Alexander approaches the problems associated with subjective experience of time by beginning with Augustine's formulation of a theory of time based on subjective experience of it, and a theory of self based on memory. Augustine's three-fold present (the present of past things, a present of present things, and a present of future things) is such that past is perceived by memory, present by direct perception, and future things by expectation. Augustine's theory of time is also a theory of selfhood according to which the self is dependent upon memory. (The continuation of consciousness is assumed.)

The solution I am promoting is a narrative variation on the three-fold present. But the past/present/future conceptualization does not necessarily carry the narrative linearly. The past is held in present consciousness, not as the past of the narrative present, but as *part of* the narrative present. For example, Alexander asks her self what it would be like to meet the Indian grandmother that she has never seen, a woman from another time and another place, on the corner of 113th Street in Manhattan. She imagines catching sight of her grandmother in the distance; she wonders what her grandmother would look like and what she, Meena, would look like through her grandmother's eyes. What would her grandmother think of her and her way of life, a half a world away from her ancestral site? And this imagining becomes part of the narrative material. It is in this way, imaginatively holding together elements of the past, and more than one narrative tradition, that culturally incompatible narratives cross over. And it is in this way that recollections from the past and anticipations about the future are held together on the "brink" of present consciousness.

The Internarrative Identity of my alternative subject is developed in the dialectic between embodiment and self-representational acts. In Ricoeur's diagram one's Narrative Identity is created in the process of dialectical mediation between *ipse* and *idem,* selfhood through commitment to permanence in time and the sameness of lasting dispositions. In my alternative diagram, one's Internarrative Identity is created in the dialectical mediation between the sameness of the body and representational possibilities.

According to Narrative Identity Theory, a whole and unified narrative is necessary for a whole and unified identity. But an Internarrative Subject has not one but several narratives (which are not mutually exclusive) and consequently has multiple selves (which are not mutually exclusive) and consequently has multiple selves (which are also not mutually exclusive). This alternative self creates her contingent identity in the narrative crossover, in the cross over from one narrative to another. That is to say that the Internarrative Subject does not identify herself with this or that narrative exclusively. Internarrative Identity is created more from the experience in margins of traditional narratives than it is by the narratives themselves.

If it is the case that there are two clearly defined structures of consciousness in the East and the West and that they are intrinsically antithical to each other, this antithesis is reflected most clearly in what is assumed to be the object of knowledge. The fundamental Western dualism between subject and object is such that conceptualization is directed at discovering, or creating, unity behind diverse phenomena. The goal is to master or control the object while not fundamentally changing the subject. In an Eastern context, knowledge is traditionally sought with the aim of altering subjective consciousness rather than controlling the external world. In the wake of Western imperialis, research into the adaptive strategies of subjects in postcolonial cultural impositions.[14] "Contextualization" is the cognitive separation of activities in which physical separation is symbolic of cultural difference. For example, Western influence has been responsible for creating a rift between the place where one works and the place where one "lives" so that modes of being at work and at home are very different. So in adapting, or "contextualizing," someone might dress for work in Western style garments, speak English, and disregard intercaste rules of association, while at home strictly observing all the traditional social codes, *without any conflict.* These compartmentalized ways of being are at odds with Western consciousness which aims at universalistic principles of behavior and could potentially cause considerable cognitive dissonance in a western subject. The Western assumption of the ego-ideal of self and identity that is overwhelmingly oriented toward inner integration and consistency, can cause problems in situations of narrative conflict. Eastern subjects often express a structuring of the self that is contextualized and highly relational so that this type of inconsistency is not a threat to "oneself."

Returning again to my alternative diagram, "self-representation" takes the place of "keeping a promise." But here "self-representation" takes the place of "keeping a promise." But here "self-representation" does not imply a unified representation. Let us look again to our example. Like Ricoeur, Alexander wonders about the sense in which the involuntary can be made meaningful through emplotment; she wonders about the boundaries of self-authorship. And to this end she looks back to her tradition to retrieve a narrative style, a "katha," with which she can imaginatively construct an identity which incorporates a past.

The Malayalam word for life-story is *"katha"* and *katha,* which is often recited in a song-like formal narration done in a standing position, differs from the Western conception of life-story in several particular ways: First, in terms of "truth value," the story is understood as a mixture of non-fiction and fabrication. Second, the role of creativity is different. The associations are more free-floating. This is poetic association. Third, they differ in the *intent* of narrating. The purpose of a katha is *not* to make sense of a life by arranging it in a pre-determined form. *Kathas* are a way of remembering; they are a way of incorporating past experiences (not just of oneself but of others as well) into one's present identity. A *katha* may, for example, establish a pattern between events that were previously unconnected. And it may, in the same recitation, sever these associations and create new ones. Fourth, *kathas* differ in the requirement of structural unity. *Kathas* do not necessarily assume Aristotelian structural requirements.

In a section of *Fault Lines* called *"Katha"* Alexander tells of being "torn apart" by two opposing yet not mutually exclusive ways of being toward the past. One way is to view the past as a place from where she came, "lives embedded in lives, rooms within rooms." The other way to regard the past is to view it as a history of existential choices. An example of a *katha* from Alexander's past which is particularly pertinent to the discussion about the link between identity, narrative unity, and dislocation, is what Alexander calls the "recognition tale." The recognition tale is not a particular story, but a series of spontaneously created stories by her father about recognizing her at various times in various places around the world.

An example of one of these types of recognition tales is one that her father tells about standing waiting on the roof of the Red Sea Hotel in order to see her ship arrive from India. The narrative describes, in intricate detail, sighting the ship in the far distance, seeing someone on deck, and recognizing it as Meena. As a child, being recognized by another as the same Meena she was before, in the previous place, saved her from a sense of utter selflessness resulting from repeated cultural dislocation. The recognition tale is not descriptive; the details are fabricated by weaving together—reassociating—recollections, experiences, events. Nor is it a unified story in the conventional sense. Without the burden of operating as concordance, a *katha* allows the teller the creative option to omit, to fabricate, to remain open-ended and continuous. In this way the meaning of an event is not dependent upon its place in the master-plot. The meaning of an event is determined by its provisional association with other events, experiences, embodied memories, kinesthetic associations.

Let me emphasize that recognition by another is not being suggested as a solution to the requirement of consistent identity, as proof of what Ricoeur terms "lasting dispositions," but rather this particular childhood *katha* is included in the memoir in order to articulate the problem and provide a solution. The *problem* is that this narrator cannot rely on any inherited sense of self bound up with the ancestral site, and the western tradition of narrative unity, as I have argued in the two previous chapters, requires too much experiential negation. The *solution* is that new and different *kathas* are created and re-created repeatedly throughout her childhood moves in order to establish a provisional self which still accounts for the past, for other lives lived. This is the opposite of an over-riding master narrative.

The crucial point is that identity does not depend upon unified narrative structure for its coherence. A subject is the "same" (*idam*) to the extent that she is embodied and has memory. And narrative retains its strength as a technique through which the subject can author herself by re-figuring the given, the involuntary.

Consistent with Ricoeur's model, my alternative represents the holding together of experience, but contrary to Ricoeur's model my brand of narrator does not hold experience together by placing it chronologically before some experience and after some other experience. In other words an alternative structure does not prioritize temporal chronology as an organizing structure. This shift is structural priority enables the non-temporally ordered association of experiences. By "non-temporally ordered" I do not mean that there can be no reference to time (there may be references to seasons, cycles, stages) but temporality is not the organizing structure.

There will be a principle of association in each narrative which may, for example, have to do with *space* and *place.*

The Internarrative Subject is not only more fully embodied than Ricoeur's conception of self, the space around the body becomes very important. A subject does not exist in despatialized time. So my narrative would be less concerned with *when* I was in India, and whether I was there before or after some other move, and more concerned with the experiences themselves. In other words, my narrative would be more concerned with *where* I have been than *when* I was there. By making *place* the structural principle one avoids Ricoeur's temporal structure which would synthesize experience into the theme: Traveling.

I have a friend who hates to go "home" to her parent's house at the other end of the country. She says that when she goes home she "becomes another person." When she is at her parent's home, she says she can't remember what is generally important to her. Certain aspects of herself just do not fit in there. She has the experience of reverting back to the little girl she was when she lived in her parent's home. This is commonly thought of as "time standing still" in a certain place, often our childhood homes.

I am suggesting that ways of being are powerfully connected to place. Temporality is one of the *least* significant orientations in my friend's experience because as a grown woman she *experiences* her childhood home the same way she did when she was a little girl. Her associations with *place* might be an important organizing principle while temporality would be less structurally important because whether my friend was twelve or twenty or thirty-five, her experience in a significant *place* has remained constant.

Meena Alexander cannot be the same person in Manhattan, New York, as she is in New Delhi, India, anymore than my friend can stop from being another self when she goes home. And not only are ways of being intricately connected to place, narrative voice changes with the location of the narrator. The woman Alexander is in various places will not fit into a unified narrative structure and to synthesize her experiences in other places would be to silence the selves she is in those other place. Again, while multiple narratives may be incommensurable (this is why Ricoeurean structure does not work) they need not be autonomous, unconnected narratives either. The project is to make connections between the lives lived in other places, with present ways of being; this is a type of narrative memory. The method of making connections between otherwise incommensurable narratives is to make Internarrative associations thereby enriching the filed of association.

Narrative Identity is consistent with an Aristotelian-based composition but my alternative compositional structure permits radical cultural change and contextual upheaval to become part of the narrative. In this sense, ones narrative can engage experiences and memories that traditional narratives skip over. This alternative structure opens up richer possibilities for the re-association of meaning, or in Ricoeurean terms, a hermeneutics of faith.[15]

What, then, do I mean by plot? First let me re-state what, in my system, it is *not*. Plot is *not* a synthesizing, unifying structure. Emplotment involves imaginatively rendering experience by ordering and re-arranging images and memories. The experience that one privileges may somehow be correlative to some tradition's sense of identity, for example, experience of the ancestral home which is correlative to the traditional Indian sense of self, and experiences of rupture which are correlated, negatively, to contemporary western Narrative Identity Theory. There *is* constraint on these alternative renderings in the sense that these images and memories are not created from nothing; they are fabricated with the threads of various experiences, kinesthetic memories, and spatial impressions. The associations are not completely fixed and they are not completely random. The Internarrative subject intends to break customary and habitual associations.

Internarrative Identity is an on-going creative attempt to avoid the restrictions of traditional plot and correlative identity structure, and equally, to avoid the simple imitation of fractured experience. Internarrative is the on-going creative ordering which resists assimulating that which it orders. The interest in telling an inclusive story does not leave the Internarrator litinizing every experience she has ever had, or every thought that enters her mind in stream-of-consciousness style. This narrator *does* marginalize some experiences, and multiple voices are variously amplified and silenced. But this marginalizing and silencing is not the result of the imposition of the canonical narrative structure. It is the result of an attempt to transcend the boundaries of traditional narrative agency.

Chapter V

Repression and Narrative Unity

The very goal of the whole process of the cure . . . is to substitute for the bits and pieces of stories that are unintelligible as well as unbearable, a coherent and acceptable story.
—Paul Ricoeur, *Time and Narrative* volume III

We trim off and discard into forgetfulness the incoherent bits that won't go into any kind of story we can tell ourselves—incoherent *because* they won't go in; that is if we notice them at all.
—Rebecca Goldstein, *The Late Summer Passion of a Woman of Mind*

As a child I survived by forgetting. Later, the amnesia became a problem as large as the one it was meant to conceal.
—Sylvia Fraser, *My Father's House*

Ideally, analysis brings it about that this concordant and discordant chorus of voices is no longer obliterated or muted by repression.
—Roy Schafer, *Retelling a Life*

At this point one might conclude that I am demonstrated the need for alternative narrative structure only for those individuals whose identity is intimately marked by more than one culture, but that I have not demonstrated any need to revise the Ricoeurean model for subjects whose identity is framed by one culture, particularly if that culture is Western. In this chapter I will argue that the need for alternative narrative structure is stronger, also impacting the lives of those subjects whose identity arises from Western culture. I will argue that the narrative requirements of unity and wholeness foster and sustain psychological repression. This sort of repression will be exemplified by the literary character of Eva Mueller. And I will refer to psychologist Roy Schafer's work on narrative in psychoanalytic settings. Then I will provide examples of narrative solutions to the sort of repression I am claiming that unified structure maintains.

I would like to begin by providing an example of the type of repression that traditional unified/whole narrative structure can, and I think regularly does, promote and maintain. The example is found in Rebecca Goldstein's *The Late Summer Passion of a Woman of Mind.*

The major character of the novel is Eva Mueller, a forty-seven-year-old philosophy professor who values abstraction, transcendence, and what she has convinced herself is, "Friendliness, not fervor. Detachment, not desire." Eva lives in her head, among the universals of Plato and Spinoza. Even her aesthetic sensibilities are not sensual, for example, her preference is for the beauty of music so harmonious that it has no sound. She is physically emaciated, and disgusted with womanhood and its "viscous pool of feelings and sensations, with nothing firm and ungiving to get a grip on."[1] Eva has not given herself over to "that insidious spread of triviality claiming the lives of most women . . . specks of pettiness, the dreary details of eating, dressing, housekeeping, shopping . . . the soggy substance of lost paludal lives."[2]

Eva Mueller is convinced that what she is engaged in is "actively seeking one's Beauty . . . reconstructing the unifying vision."[3] But the narrator calls what Eva engages in self-deception. In fact, the novel opens with the words: "We are all masters of self deception." Eva has engaged in a long and arduous process of self deception which has required what she considers an "ethics of detachment,"

> For there is salvation in the liberation of the self from the self. Sink one's sight in what is—austere and remote—and one's attachment to the particular—the personal and the petty—will wither away. This is the attitude of high-mindedness, the ethics of detachment.[4]

The dominant narrative (along with the fact that the author's previous novel was entitled, and concerned, *The Mind Body Problem*) suggests that the protagonist's denial of the body and everything associated with it (the specific, passions, contingency, the passing of time) is the result of the unconscious presence of guilt for her father's involvement with the Nazis' The repression of the horrors of war that she witnessed, and feels partially responsible for, has required that Eva shut down that part of herself with which she feels—her body. The Eva Mueller we meet at the beginning of the novel, *in media res,* is a middle-aged philosophy professor who has no memory of the faces of the Jewish children she watched being loaded in the trains headed for the camps. And as the novel unfolds we learn that during her years in graduate school her unconscious guilt impelled her into a relationship with a sadistic Jewish man, an experience she also represses. But in the "present" of the novel Eva Mueller is not the same person she was in graduate school nor is she her father's daughter. She is, "different, in the most fundamental sense possible, from the vast majority of others. From her own past self. This distinction had been her very end."[5] But the problem is that the intentional disassociation of her past selves from the self she has created anew, has left Eva nearly past-less and close to disembodied.

What is the salvation of Eva Mueller? The novel's dominant narrative seems to answer, "love." Love induces a release of the physical and all that is associated with it; and the integration of the mind and the previously repressed body enables the release of memories. As in *Fault Lines,* embodied memory is represented as the place where the past resides. When Eva falls in love, with someone who is interested in both Spinoza and rock and roll, she becomes much more sensually attuned. For example, she begins to appreciate music that is audible. And suddenly her perceptions are not limited to the cognitive. She develops a friendship with a woman sociology professor who she used to find repulsive. Eva had always been uncomfortably aware of this woman's femininity, earthiness, and sense of humor, but suddenly in tandem with conscious embodiment, she realized something she hadn't before—this woman is Jewish.

The novel ends with a physical joining of Eva and the man she lives, and simultaneous with this consummation is a flood of memories, memories that are drastically inconsistent with the ones she had previously allowed herself. She suddenly remembers her father's face. But it was not the kind wise face she was so familiar with, it was an ugly face that was hard and bitter when he spoke about the ones he hated. She remembers her father's words, which "dripped with poison . . . the words of a bad man."[6]

But I would like to suggest a more nuanced reading than the "solution" of the novel's dominant narrative. Mine is an alternative to the interpretation which describes what Eva Mueller has as a mind/body problem, which is alleviated by the integration of the two, enabled by love. I am suggesting that Eva's salvation will be achieved when she voices the selves and experiences that had been silenced by an assumed narrative structure. The way I read it, Eva's repression is not primarily physical. The regression of the body is simply, or not so simply, her chosen *method* of repression of the multiplicity of who she had been and what she has done. The narrator herself provides another way to read Eva's story, an alternative to the Master-narrative, when she says,

> We live our lives by telling ourselves stories . . . our human creativity is, for the most part, exercised not in the production of new forms but rather in the finding of ways to force our material into the finite available few. We trim off and discard into forgetfulness the incoherent bits that won't go into any kind of story we can tell ourselves—incoherent *because* they won't go in; that is if we notice them at all.[7]

Now to further my argument that the achievement of narrative unity is an achievement is psychological repression I would like to make use of the contributions of narrative psychologist Roy Schafer. Then I will return to the example of

Eva Mueller. Schafer provides a theoretical model of discordance-inclusive stories and subjects which counters Ricoeur's conception of coherent intelligible subjectivity. His work describes the problems associated with representing a singular self in a unified narrative.

Like Ricoeur, or most any Narrative Identity theorist, Schafer assumes that "the self is always a narrative construction," that identity is dependent upon the storyline one sees oneself as a part of, and that how a life story is told depends upon the contexts and interests of the narrator. He assumes that we are at least partial authors of our lives, "an author of existence is someone who constructs experience. Experience is something that is made or fashioned; it is not encountered, discovered, or observed except on secondary reflection."[8]

> The so-called self may be considered to be a set of narrative strategies or storylines each person follows in trying to develop an emotionally coherent account of his or her life among people. We organize our past and present experiences narratively.[9]

Narrative is not an alternative to truth or reality; it is the mode in which truth and reality are presented. There are only versions, and narratively unmediated truth or reality is impossible. In the psychoanalytic setting. Schafer says, the analyst must constantly ask herself "of what story or stories is this a part, and for what constructive purpose is it being re-told?" But then Schafer concerns himself with something Ricoeur doesn't.

Schafer is interested in describing the problems that occur when the multiplicity of narrated selves is diminished and reduced in order to represent a singular self which can fit a unified culturally imposed story line. On this account, similar to Ricoeur's and Alexander's account, the psychoanalytic telling is not a process through which the self is uncovered, but a process in which self is constructed. And the requirement for narrative unity is identified as the basis for repression of discordant experience. What Schafer calls a "storyline" is what I call an assumed narrative structure. It is a,

set of guidelines and constraints for telling a story that conveys what convention would certify as having a certain general kind of content . . . and through reduction, to create faithful repetitions of these versions out of apparently diverse narrative materials.[10]

While Ricoeur equates selfhood with a unified narrative, Schafer equates psychologically healthy selfhood with the expression of multiple voices, selves, and discordant experiences,

> the crucial analytic versions tell of a multitude of voices rising from his or her own imagined inner world. Ideally, analysis brings it about that this concordant and discordant chorus of voices is no longer obliterated or muted by repression.

Schafer opposes the Ricoeurean view of self which establishes a narrative of basic mental unity. On that very ricoeurean model, the model of mental unity,

> this entity (the self) is presented as retaining its identity over time and even though every one of its elements may change, and it is supposedly capable of regaining its mature identity after it has lost it through stress-induced regression.[11]

What Schafer is attacking is precisely that which Ricoeur promotes as a model of ethical selfhood (*ipse*) which is evidenced by the act of keeping a promise in spite of changes in conditions. It is the type of self is created through its "challenge to time . . . denial of change."[12]

When Ricoeur illustrates his concept of narrative identity by returning to the experience of psychoanalysis in which the analysand creates herself in the process of telling her story, he emphasizes the parallel between the manipulation of the narrative component in psychoanalytic telling, and poetic composition, "the very goal of the whole process of the cure . . . is to substitute for the bits and pieces of stories that are unintelligible as well as unbearable, a coherent and acceptable story."[13] And recall that homophony is one of the requirements of an "acceptable" and "coherent" narrative identity. But Schafer argues that, "those analysts who insist that there is only a single self . . . do not recognize that they are making a narrative choice."[14] While the Ricoeurean view of the self has been the dominant psychological narrative, Schafer favors the type of stories which do not silence experiences which do not fit a unified structure, ultimately insisting that,

> self-deception is but one instance of a set of problematic ideas that are introduced by self theorists or grand self narratives. It is advantageous to regard self-deception as a story that people tell in order to present themselves or make a psychoanalytic interpretation . . . it is a story that 'works': It communicates effectively and it helps construct experience. But it only one version.[15]

In order for Eva Mueller to achieve the construction of a unified identity, she had to repress, to "discard," that experiential material that did not "fit" into the whole/unified narrative structure. She strives for a pure vision, like her aesthetic sensibility, a unified story. Eva has repressed lots of potential narrative material and her past selves and experiences have little to do with who she is now. Her narrative achievement has been an achievement in psychological repression.

The narrator comments on the consequences of applying a classical aesthetic principle to our personal stories when she observes that, "The aesthetic preference for wholeness will often lead us to actions we would not otherwise undertake. . . ."[16] These are not only the "actions" of narrating a story in accordance with the rules, but the "actions" are also those which are a *result* of the "aesthetic preference for wholeness." This is the aesthetic preference which led Eva Mueller to involve herself in a relationship with a sadistic Jewish man who engages in semi-unconscious revenge against her for what his family has suffered. As the narrator says, "It's these internal reconstructions that *determine their actions,* which is why the narrative mode is more suited for the explanation of human behavior than some more straightforwardly causal account." And, she says, "One has to recapture the agent's telling in order to grasp the significance of his or her action; that is, to provide the matrix for saying what, in fact, the action was."[17] There are "underlying stories generating the actions."[18] The first time Eva met Martin Weltbaum, she knew that he was Jewish. "It had amazed her as a child when, sometimes, as her mother and she were waling in the city, they would pass someone and her mother would whisper, 'Jew.' How could she always tell?" But Eva, the graduate student in philosophy knew, like her mother, the first time she laid eyes on Martin Weltbaum. Something in her head whispered, "Jew."

Armed with her aesthetic convictions, Eva sets out on a quest for unity, assumes classical plot structure and goes about repressing certain experiences, and privileging and creating stories around other experiences. As the narrator says,

> There are some general rules we employ in going about making up the stories we tell about ourselves . . . principles of aesthetics . . . for we are, none of us, completely indifferent to the claims of Beauty in the telling of our tales. Take, for example, the profound pleasure we derive in the apprehension of a whole, which is, as Aristotle tells us in the *Poetics,* with staggering simplicity, 'what has a beginning a middle, and an end.'[19]

What kind of story can the guilt-ridden daughter of a Nazi tell herself? The story that Eva told for a long time synthesized an initial familial harmony, with tension and conflict in the middle, a concluding reconciliation in the form of a union between a Nazi's daughter and a survivor's son, and the restoration of initial balance with the birth of their child to stabilize the ending. What Goldstein calls an aesthetic preference for wholeness, and what I call a tacitly assumed aesthetic structure, leads Eva Mueller into this relationship and then provides her with reasons to stay. Other experiences in Eva's life drop away, as maintaining her story, and its implied structure, become the most important activity she engages in. When eventually she becomes pregnant, she feels that the child was "meant to be" and in a prototypical-narrative it would be. As Ricoeur says:

> Because of the concordant-discordant synthesis, the contingency of an event contributes to the necessity, retroactive so to speak, of a history of a life, to which is equated the identity of the character. Thus chance is transmuted to fate. And the identity of the character so emplotted, so to speak, can only be understood in terms of this dialectic.[20]

But the problem is that while Eva has been participating in one story, the man she is involved with is telling himself a different story and he does not share her aesthetic preference. The shattering realization of the part she played in *his* story is the catalyst which changed Eva into the person she is now.

> Eva had constructed a very good tale indeed about her relationship with Martin Weltbaum, fraught with moral import, as are all the best narratives—for the aesthetic sensibility has a great affinity with the moral. And then she had caught the drift of *his* version.[21]

She caught the drift of his version when she told him that she was pregnant with his child. His reaction was extremely violent and before leaving her he screamed out *his* version of the story. The story he had been telling himself was one of revenge. According to him, they were not Eva and Martin involved in a relationship, they were a Nazi's daughter and a Jew. Since the shock of hearing his version of the story, she has become the other Eva, the detached abstract Eva Mueller we meet at the beginning of the novel. And since then Eva has had to create another story.

But Eva's crucial mistake, I think, is an aesthetic one. Her failing is to create another story while maintaining the same old structure. Now the task of creating a whole/unified plot has become even more demanding as the narrative material has become increasingly diverse. Eva no longer sees herself as part of that past story, but how can she tell a unified/whole narrative which accounts for her past and yet adequately represents her current situation?

Eva's imagination fails her and she complies with classical structural demands and once again represses the parts of her experience that won't fit into any "coherent" story she can tell about herself. The crucial moment for change was the moment of narrative conflict, the moment when she realized the part she played in *his* story. This was one of those jarring, potentially life-changing moments, internal earthquakes, which may cause one to reflect over who one is and what one has done. To see the story she is involved in through the eyes of *another* was shock enough to make Eva want to extricate herself rom this story completely. But this jolting insight had the potential to be so much more for Eva. This narrative conflict was an opportunity to uncover what she had repressed, but Eva didn't even ask herself how she ended up in a situation like this. There was no attempt to glean any larger insight. She simply wanted to end that story and start another one, and the narrative tradition she had inherited provided her with the means to do that.

Quite the opposite of enabling her to make sense of the events of her life, traditional structure has enabled, and helps maintain, Eva's repression. To argue this is not to argue that there is a direct causal connection between classical structural requirements and repression, but there *is* a symbiotic relationship between the two. Eva's aesthetic preference, a preference shared by her culture, assists, fosters, and maintains her repression.

Much like Meena Alexander, Eva Mueller experiences narrative conflict but her conflict is not cross-cultural; it is the conflict of her narrative *with the narrative of another*. Her solution is simply to "trim off," to "discard" the selves she has been and the experiences she has had that won't fit into any *unified* story she can tell about herself.

In the previous chapter I advocated an alternative narrative model, one that would engender an alternative subjectivity. My alternative model involves not one but multiple narratives, not one but multiple voices. And it involves what I have termed "Internarrative associations." Eva's Internarrative Identity, on my model, would be created in the process of mediating self and sameness, *aham* and *idam,* and the body with self representation. This alternative narrative model would enable Eva Mueller to integrate her pasts with her present. But "integrate" as I use it here, does not imply unification or synthesis. It means that Eva could *variously* include parts of her past in her present narrative. It means that the pieces of her life that won't fit into a unified narrative *can* be narrated in a story which is not unified. My alternative model would not require Eva to repress but it would allow her to consciously decide to include or exclude, privilege or marginalize, any part that she chooses to, in any particular telling.

The narrative solution for Eva Mueller would have been to do what Meena Alexander has done. Eva should begin by allowing all her voices to speak. She should let the Nazi's daughter speak; she should let the masochistic graduate student speak. The detached disembodied professor Eva Mueller should also be voiced. She should narrate all the selves she has been in various places at various times. *And then she should associate Internarratively.* This would be a never-ending process. it is this on-going process of narratively mediating her self-centralization and her sameness with others, of mediating the involuntary (the body) with agency (self-representation) that she will create her ever-changing Internarrative Identity. This narrative mediation, of course, is not structured in the same old way. Each of the multiple narratives will have some structure, if structure means the on-going process of giving meaning to experience by associating with other experiences. it is my claim that in this process of creating Internarrative associations identity is created.

Consider again my alternative Internarrative model:

Maan

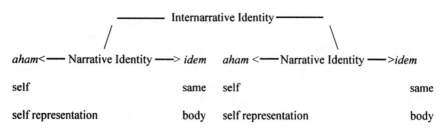

In this model, the consistency of the self does not depend upon a unified narrative structure for its coherence. The subject is the "same" subject as a result of memory and embodiment, *not* as a result of commitment to say the same as Ricoeur would have it. Eva's narratives are all housed in one body. The body is the constant; it remains. It has, like Ricoeur's tool, an "enduring overall structure" *and* it is the locus of another type of permanence in time because it houses kinesthetic memory. Remember Alexander's insistence that "The structures of human memory bear with them the imprint of the spatial existence of the lived body through which alone they have been generated,"[22] such that the burden of holding together discordant experience need not be shouldered by a unified narrative structure, because embodied memory holds them together. In the same sense embodied memory and narrative unity seem almost antithical. Ricoeur thinks that we need a method for making sense of experience in its multiplicity. Unified narrative structure is his method of "synthesizing discordant experience" but as I have argued with the example of *Fault Lines* this method requires the silencing of types of experience which may otherwise be central to one's story. And this silencing or repression becomes a problem itself as we see in the example of Eva Mueller. Eva Mueller's repression is important because without it she would be unable to achieve an over-riding narrative which unifies her experience, a narrative which creates the appearance of sameness from the beginning to the end.

The alternative to a unified and whole structure is the narration of multiple narratives and imaginatively creating Internarrative associations. Similar to Alexander's imagining her grandmother in contemporary New York, Eva Mueller could imagine, for example, the "self" she was in graduate school meeting the "self" she was as her father's daughter. She could imagine Eva the graduate student catching sight of Eva the little girl, in the distance. What would Eva the little girl look like through the eyes of Eva the graduate student? Would she see the guilt, humiliation, confusion? And how would Eva the graduate student seem through the eyes of Eva the little girl? It is in this way, imaginatively holding together and re-associating elements of the past selves, that narratives cross over. *And* it is in the way that memory is kept on the "brink" of present consciousness, *and* it is in this way that meaning is re-configured.

Contemporary discussions concerning Narrative Identity among Ricoeur scholars have not accounted for the aesthetic criteria that I am claiming is at the foundation of Ricoeurean personal identity. In order to argue this point I will look to the work of Ricoeur scholar Morny Joy because the assumptions she makes are representative of the aesthetic oversight I am claiming is prevalent in Ricoeur scholarship,[23] and because this oversight has important implications.[24]

Joy is interesting to me because she finds in Ricoeur the solution to her attempts to locate a form of feminist subjectivity, which is neither the fractured subject a' la postmodernism, nor the Enlightenment's autonomous individual. But Joy makes some crucially mistaken assumptions that I would like to uncover as they underscore my thesis.

In "Writing as Repossession"[25] Morny Joy is interested in demonstrating the "artifices of idealization and impartiality" of what she describes as the predominantly male approach to personal narration, and yet she is not interested in the other extreme—complete fragmentation. Joy resonates with Kristeva's idea of a "polymorphous perversity that delights in its own indeterminancy," and yet she finds that the position Kristeva endorses leaves women in a purely reactionary position. Women's marginal status is potentially disruptive and destabilizing, but Joy worries that, on Kristeva's view, one's marginal position can register protest but not effect change.[26] Shari Benstock's view[27] is more constructive but still "suspicious." Instead of indulging in the disjuncture that Kristeva advocates, Benstock explores the reasons for the disjuncture. Her awareness of the self as a construct does not lead to relativism but to an awareness of the details that create the construct. In her search for a middle ground, between postmodern fragmentation and the modernist self, Joy looks to Ricoeur and finds a solution in his conception of narrative identity.

What appeals to Joy about Ricoeurean narrative identity is the attention to the nuances of the interplay between *idem* and *ipse*, the emphasis on the specific or contextually dependent sense of self, and the manner in which narrative mediation allows one to name and claim aspects of one's life. Joy is interested in Ricoeur's insistence on the capacity of narrative to account for the contexts within which identity has meaning. Equally compelling is the idea of narrative as technique or as agency. But Joy looks to Ricoeur to find a sense of identity that an already marginal female subject can access, without adequate consideration of the structural dimension of this form of identity. This oversight leaves her solution partial. While I agree that narrative identity does provide a solution to the problem Joy is working on, I want to argue that if the category of narrative were liberalized, the solution Joy finds in Ricoeur would be complete.

Joy is disturbed by the postmodern declaration of the displacement of self just when women were assuming some form of autonomy and taking responsibility for self definition. She voices the common feminist concerns with delineating a place and space from which a woman can speak and with the notion of responsibility in light of social constructivist theories of subjectivity. Joy wonders about the options left for a woman who seeks to tell her life story: "What sense of self can she claim if she is not to succumb to the temptations of either an idealized univocal self or to any number of heterogeneous guises in the name of an unstable postmodern subject?"[28] she looks to narrative identity as a way out of this impasse. But almost immediately after importing Ricoeur to solve her problem she apologizes for the "past associations narrative seems to have with predominantly linear and logical procedures" and offers the term "strategic" in its place. Thereafter narrative identity and strategic identity are used interchangeably. Joy "would prefer to use the term strategic identity, but the process is the same. This term alludes to the fact that to narrate ones life is always an interpretation, situated at the confluence of many influences." But her conception of strategic identity and Ricoeur's conception of narrative identity are not interchangeable. The associations that narrative has with "linear and logical procedures" are an essential aspect of Ricoeur's conception of "narrative." In fact, as I've argued in preceding chapters, Ricoeur intentionally and methodically remains faithful to the these procedures as they are essential for Ricoeur's connection between time and narrative.[29] The substitution of terms, however, evidences the discomfort with the narrative structure that Ricoeur as insists upon. And it is for sound reason that Joy is uncomfortable. Her thesis is that a female subject can narratively appropriate the involuntary aspects of experience, but within Ricoeur's model, this thesis can work only if Joy substitutes her own terms and aesthetic requirements. While I share the inclination to broaden the Ricoeurean conception of emplotment, the type of substitution Joy engages in is not unproblematic.

Joy misinterprets Ricoeur's saying that: "We learn to become the narrator of our own story without becoming the author of our life" as a statement about a type of perspective which enables one to think of identity as a construct that allows for change as a result of critical self-awareness. She reads Ricoeur's statement as a rejection of Master-plot or Master-narrative, "At any one time . . . I could be trying to grasp or make sense of a particular episode that has affected my life, in relation to other plots, rather than writing an all-embracing panorama that incorporates every aspect of my existence."[30] But this statement is not interpreted in the context of Ricoeur's larger project. When he says "we learn to become the narrator of our own story without becoming the author of our life" Ricoeur means that narrative identity mediates between social construction and self determination. Narrative is a method of taking control of what one is given. Narrative identity is Ricoeur's solution to the problems initially raised in *Freedom and Nature: The Voluntary and the Involuntary.* A plot operates as glue between the flux of experiences that threaten to overwhelm us. To emplot oneself is to thematize events; it is to make sense of the involuntary. it is also the manner in which will can be exerted over the determined.[31] It is the voluntary means by which the involuntary can be made meaningful. The notion of "authoring" one's existence does not adequately account for the social/cultural/contextual aspects of identity formation, but to *re*-tell, to "*co*-author," the given is to appropriate the involuntary.

To further her argument Joy investigates the narratives of three women, all three are incest survivors. The three works are: *Don't: A Woman's Word* by Elly Danica,[32] *Daddy's Girl* by Charlotte Vale Allen,[33] and *My Father's House* by Sylvia Fraser.[34] Joy's argument is that Ricoeur's conception of Narrative Identity is a solution to the violations these women have suffered in the past. By re-telling the involuntary, by assigning alternative meaning to it, they exert some measure of agency. But, as I will demonstrate, at least two of these three narratives go further than Joy accounts for. And the reason that they are successful is that they *do not* comply with Ricoeurean aesthetic demands. These stories are not unified or whole. They are not monological. And yet they are not fragmentary or disassociate. The narratives are an attempt to *integrate* past experiences with present ways of being.

I point to Joy's oversight in order to better flesh out my problem with, and solution to, Ricoeur's notion of Narrative Identity. The problem is the restrictive definition of narrative, and the solution, the solution executed by at least two of these narrators, is to radicalize an inherited sense of narrative. Theirs are still identities even though they are not singular, unified, nor whole. What Joy wants to dispense with, "the linearity and logical procedures" of narrative, are, for Ricoeur, essential features of narrative intelligibility and its correlative coherent identity. The structuring procedure (*muthos*) is the Aristotelian one.[35]

Let me go further in focusing on the problem and the solution these narratives provide. Joy observes that in all three of these narratives, the focus is on a particular trauma to the exclusion of all else.[36] And this exclusion makes incest the dominant narrative. These women are attempting, narratively, to come to terms with, and exert some control over, their pasts. But I think there is more. These narrators seem to want to integrate the experiences that have been repressed with the rest of their consciously remembered past. For example, Fraser says,

> My life was structured on the uncovering of a mystery. As a child I survived by
> forgetting. Later, the amnesia became a problem as large as the one it was meant
> to conceal.[37]

And Allen tells of feeling herself split into what she terms "the one" and "the other." The extreme split between the private self and public self is something she was unable to integrate until she narrated her stories. Their writing has enabled these women to recuperate "a part of their lives that was lost or relegated to an inaccessible file."[38] It has enabled them to attempt an integration between the stories they have been telling themselves and others (the public), and the experiences they have repressed (the private). Narrating their lives is an enabler *because* these women transform traditional structure.

The previously unified stories these women told were enabled by the repression required by traditional structure. The "coherent" story had required the repression that I have claimed the whole/unified structure demands. But this repression, which Frazer addresses directly, has itself become a problem. Subverting traditional structure is their attempt to allow repressed experience back into consciousness and into the stories they tell about themselves.

I find Joy's reading of Frazer and Danica problematic because she overlooks the narrative agency these women have taken; she does not seem to grasp the technique that makes their narratives work. For example, Danica's story is not temporally organized, nor is it homophonic, continuous or whole. In fact, the narrative is made up of paragraphs numbered from 1.1 to, fifty-two pages later, 13.6. The narrative does not go from childhood forward. It does not begin *en media res*. The entries are not chronologically arranged. Sometimes seasons are mentioned but these seasons are not cyclical; they do not function as the temporal string that holds the pieces of narrative together. Le me provide a sample of this writing style. The first words with which this narrative begins are.

> 1.1 DON'T. I only know this word. This is the only word I have ever learned. Don't. I can not write with only this word. A woman's vocabulary: Don't
> 1.2 Don't tell. Don't think. Don't whatever you do, don't feel. If you feel pain the pain will be there again. Don't.

And so the narrative goes on. The last words are these:

> 13.6 Survival. Dreaming with a pen in my hand. Writing. Writing. Writing. Who will hear me?

This narrative is not at all incoherent although it is not temporally organized nor unified nor whole.

All three of these women experience the narrative conflict they describe as the conflict between private and public selves, the private selves having been previously repressed. But the narratives that Joy examines are narratives of cross-over, they are inter-narratives between public and private selves. These narratives involve both spheres variously incorporated. These women create their provisional identities by narratively mediating the sameness of their embodied selves and memories with the agency of self representation. The public self had previously been a unified representation and the private self had been previously repressed as it, the private, was the discordant experience. By liberalizing the structures of their narratives they are able to tell a story about themselves which is inclusive of even the discordant experience so that these narratives represent the cross-over of the public narrative and the previously repressed private narrative. What I am suggesting is that the act of radicalizing inherited structure has enabled these women, Frazer and Danica, to tell narratives that are inclusive of all the experiences that will not fit into any "coherent" story they can tell about themselves. Narrating has been the transformative element for these women and non-adherence to structural codes has enabled them to narrate without silencing discordant experience. In fact, voicing the private experience, discordant experience, is what makes these narratives work. It is precisely what makes these narratives self-constitutive. Structural liberalization allows these narratives to include what the prototypical structure would synthesize, or silence.

I agree with Joy's thesis that "neither a theory of ideal types nor one of totally dislocated subjects is appropriate,"[39] but in Ricoeur she finds a solution to the feminism/postmodernism debate which is itself problematic. I locate a solution in an *extension* of Ricoeur's Narrative Identity Theory, in what I call Internarrative Identity.

In another more recent article, "Feminism and the Self,"[40] Joy blames Derridean deconstruction and the Foucaultean reduction of the subject to a function of discourse for the status of the subject in contemporary thought, and she looks toward French feminists for an alternative way to view the subject. While she finds Kristeva's continued dispersion and Irigaray's jouissance initially seductive, Joy voices a concern common among feminists, that when theory comes to practice, these ideas are somewhat wanting.[41] Kristeva's identification of postmodern dislocation with women's marginal status and Irigaray's idea of evoking feminine sensuousness and linguistic extravagances are viewed by Joy as theoretically self-indulgent and an evasion of practical responsibility. Irigaray is charged with essentialism because she comes dangerously close to identifying women with their bodies and with their pleasures alone. "Womenspeak" is Irigaray's term for the identification of women with their bodies and the self description that comes from this embodiment. But Joy worries that "women's sex and texts are so identified that this supposedly free-ranging female risks being coffined to a specific ambience of rhetorical posturing where her activity is virtually circumscribed by traditional "feminine" limitations.[42] Kristeva the "feminine" is gender-neutral, but it always a marginal category. On this model, women can be subversive within the semiotic ambience of maternity but in this case the subversive mother is the only model for women to contest their status.

Joy compares and contrasts North American and French feminist theory on the issue of identity. She wonders whether a woman's marginal status actually serves to put her in a privileged position for subversion, as Kristeva suggests? Does Irigaray's identification of women with their bodies and pleasures create an essentialism? Does a woman's standpoint make her superior in her insights into social reality as Hartsock insists? The result of a survey of recent scholarship on subjectivity including an overview of Derrida, Foucault, Kristeva, Irigaray, Gilligan, Hartsock, bell hooks, and Biddy Martin, is a return to Ricoeur for a way out of the current feminist debate concerning the possibility for female subjectivity. Joy wants to incorporate a hermeneutic practice which she sees as an example of a contextual way of knowing. She wants to extend the hermeneutic exercise from a textual exercise to a *contextual* exercise. Joy thinks, given the contemporary dilemmas, that narrative identity as a hermeneutic exercise is particularly appropriate. Her thesis is that a narrative self representation can include ambiguities and discordance without being ambiguous and discordant itself:

> a feminist writer can mirror the conflicts involved, (in self-representation) but this does not mean that the resultant delineation need be confused, that the self be beset by antagonistic impulses, or overwhelmed by conditions beyond one's control. Such a compromise bespeaks continual adherence to a male model of normative diagnosis—whether modern or postmodern.[43]

The quality that distinguishes a feminist autobiography is that it will always be marked by critical engagement with those structures which operate to contain her story.

In "feminism and the Self" Joy does not read Ricoeur as envisioning a life composed of many plots as she did in "Repossession." In the more recent article she reads his statement about being the narrator of one's life without being the author of one's existence, the way I do. Her reading has changed considerably from the earlier reading as she now wants to "expand Ricoeur's notion of a single plot to a composite of many plots." In "Repossession" I think the reason for her misreading of Ricoeur is that she does not consider his work on identity in the context of his larger project. But in her later work she amends what she argued previously and as a result of this changed understanding, she wants to "expand" his notion. But, as I have argued throughout this dissertation, to "expand" Ricoeur in the manner she suggests is to completely undermine the aesthetic conviction which is the basis of his narrative identity. Joy's impulse is similar to my own but she does not follow through on examining the results of such an expansion for narrative identity. Ricoeur's project is larger than a theory of identity. it starts out being a problem of free will or determinism. Then the project becomes a solution to Augustine's problem of temporal discordance with the imposition of Aristotelian compositional structure (*muthos*). And the solution turns out to be much more. Joy feels Ricoeur's model "has insights to offer about how we might begin to formulate notions of self-understanding in the contemporary feminist debate."[44] But, as I said before, there is tension between Ricoeur's claims to have renounced any notion of the Supreme or Master-plot, and his hermeneutic practices. However, even if one is generous with Ricoeur and reads him as assuming multiple plots rather than a Master plot (this is Joy's original reading which she amends in more recent articles) my argument about *structure* is applicable even to the generous reading. Even the structure of each one of the supposed multiple plots is Aristotelian in form.[45]

The result of overlooking the structural requirements of Ricoeurean "narrative" has been to undermine Joy's understanding of the ways in which the subjects of her study have asserted their agency by subverting Ricoeurean exclusionary requirements.

In summary, I have attempted to argue that the achievement of narrative unity, the fulfillment of classical aesthetic requirements for narrative form upon which coherent identity rests, fosters and maintains a process of psychological repression. The distinction between imaginative personal narratives and irrational or incoherent narratives, *is a structural distinction.*

Ricoeur argues that if we hope to make sense of our lives at all, if our lives are to be more than a series of disconnected atomic events, there must be narrative synthesis. On this model, the unifying synthesizing mechanism of traditional plot structure is the basis for rational coherent subjectivity. But I have attempted to problematize this mechanism and I have traced the requirement of narrative unity as the foundation for personal identity to a classic aesthetic principle.

Following Ricoeur, I've argued that who one is and what one will do will be determined by the story one sees oneself as a part of. Going further than Ricoeur, I have suggested that a genuinely imaginative theory of narrative identity would be inclusive of alternatively structured narratives. And I have argued that the assumed classical narrative structure is responsible for repression of certain *types* of experience. I used the character of Eva Mueller as an example of how the "aesthetic preference for wholeness will lead us to actions we would not otherwise undertake" and as an example of subjectivity that narrative unity produces. This is a subjectivity that requires repression for its intelligibility, rationality, coherence. Then, I introduced the psychoanalytic perspective of Roy Schafer because he is uncomfortable with the same aspect of narrative identity theory that I am concerned with—that is—the repression required in order to represent a singular self in a unified narrative. Morny Joy's work was introduced for two reasons. First, because among contemporary Ricoeur scholars her work comes closest to aspects of Ricoeurean identity that I am interested in; and second, because her oversights are representative of the prevailing understanding of Ricoeur's narrative identity.

Narrative identity theory claims that narrative will determine what our experience is, how we tell our stories, who we are, and to a large extent, what we will do. Because I agree, I want to add that the way in which the content is told, the structure of the narrative, is an essential aspect of the narrative function. The *structure* of our stories will determine what our experience is, how we tell our stories, who we are, and what our future actions may be. But meaningful narrative agency is limited by an inherited sense of narrative form. To unbind that structure is to assert agency in determining, and re-determining, who we are and what we will do, in a way that is truly imaginative.

Notes

Introduction

1. Barthes, Roland. "The Death of the Author," *Image-Music-Text.* ed. Stephen Heath (New York: Hill and Wang). 1977.
2. Foucault, Michel. "What is an Author?" *Language, Counter-Memory, Practice: Selected Essays and Interviews,* ed. Donald Bouchard. (Ithaca: Cornell University Press). 1977.
3. *Men in Feminism,* ed. Alice Jardine and Paul Smith. (New York: Methuen). 1987. pp. 231-41.
4. Johnson, Mark. *Moral Imagination: Implications of Cognitive Science for Ethics.* (Chicago: University of Chicago Press). 1993. 155.
5. Ricoeur, Paul. *Time and Narrative,* vol. I trans. Kathleen McLaughlin and David Pellauer. (Chicago: University of Chicago Press). 1983. 41.
6. *Women's Autobiography: Essays in Criticism,* ed. Estelle C. Jelinek. (Bloomington, Indiana: Indiana University Press). 1980. 17-19.
7. Ostriker, Alicia. "Thieves of Language: Female Poets and Revisionist Mythmaking" *Signs* 8 1982. 72.
8. DuPlessis, Rachel. "For the Etruscans" *The New Feminist Criticism: Essays on Women, Literature, and Theory,* ed. Elaine Showalter (New York: Pantheon Books). 1985. 243-70.
9. Showalter, Elaine. "Feminist Criticism in the Wilderness" *The New Feminist Criticism: Essays on Women, Literature, and Theory,* ed Elaine Showalter (New York: Pantheon Books). 1985. 243-70.
10. Aisenberg, Nadya. *Ordinary Heroines.* (New York, New York: Continuum Publishing Company). 1994.
11. quoted in Katz-Stoker, Fraya, "Feminism v. Formalism" *Images of Women.* Cornilleon. 323.
12. Goldstein, Rebecca. *The Late Summer Passion of a Woman of Mind.* (New York: Farrar, Straus, and Giroux). 1989. 57.
13. Alexander, Meena. *Fault Lines.* (New York: Feminist Press). 1993.

Chapter I

1. Ricoeur, Paul. *Oneself as Another.* trans. Kathleen Blamey (Chicago: University of Chicago Press) 1992.
2. Ibid. 56.
3. Ricoeur, Paul. "Narrative Identity" *Philosophy Today.* (Spring. 1991) 76.
4. *Oneself as Another.* 27.

5. Ibid. 61.
6. *The Philosophy of Paul Ricoeur: An Anthology of His Work.* ed. Charles Degan and David Steward. (Beacon Press: Boston). 1978. 199.
7. *Oneself as Another.* 200.
8. Here Ricoeur borrows from, and is in complete agreement with, Michael Sherwood, *Logic of Explanation in Psychoanalysis.* (Academic Press: New York). 1969.
9. *Oneself as Another.* 200.
10. Ibid. 22.
11. Ibid. 302.
12. Ibid. 21.
13. Ibid. 129.
14. Ibid. 118.
15. Ibid. 119.
16. Ibid. 124.
17. Ibid. 124.
18. Ibid.
19. Ibid. 165-66.
20. Ibid. 172.
21. Ibid. 221.
22. Ricoeur restricts his use of the notion of "ethics" to the societal or institutional. And he uses "moral" for interpersonal contexts.
23. *Oneself as Another.* 266.
24. Ibid. 267.
25. Ibid. 254-55.
26. Ibid. 273
27. Ibid. 141.
28. Ibid.
29. *Time and Narrative.* II. 158.
30. *Time and Narrative.* I. 35.
31. *Time and Narrative.* II. 159.
32. Ibid. 20.
33. Ibid.
34. Ibid. 22.
35. Ibid. 96-97.
36. Ibid. 96.
37. Ibid.
38. *Time and Narrative.* I. 36.
39. *Oneself as Another.* 141.
40. Ibid. 147-48.
41. Ibid. 143.
42. *Oneself as Another.* 158-59.
43. Ibid. 162.
44. *Time and Narrative.* II. 22.
45. Ibid. 97.
46. Ricoeur, Paul. *Time and Narrative.* vol. II, trans. Kathleen McLaughlin and David Pellauer. (Chicago: University of Chicago Press). 1985. 96.
47. Ibid. 97.
48. Ibid. 158.

49. Ibid. 148-49.
50. Ricoeur insists that narratives do not concern themselves with what "the hero did between events." *Time and Narrative.* I. 39.
51. *Oneself as Another.* 124.
52. Ibid.
53. Gilbert, Sandra and Susan Gubar. *No Man's Land: The Place of the Woman Writer in the Twentieth Century.* (New Haven: Yale University Press). 1990.
54. Showalter, Elaine. "Toward a Feminist Poetics," *The New Feminist Criticism: Essays on Women, Literature and Theory.* ed. Elaine Showalter. (New York: Pantheon Books). 1985. 125-143.
    see also: Walker, Nancy A. *Feminist Alternatives: Irony and Fantasy in the Contemporary Novel by Women.* (Jackson: University of Mississippi Press). 1990.
55. Brownstein, Rachel M. Becoming *a Heroine* (New York: Penguin). 1984.
56. Gubar, Susan. "Mother, Maiden, Marriage of Death."
57. Miller, Nancy K. "Emphasis Added: Plots and Plausibilities in Women's Fiction" *The New Feminist Criticism.* ed. Elaine Showalter. (New York: Pantheon Books). 1985. 339-360.
    see also: Gubar, Susan. "'The Blank Page' and Issues of Female Creativity" *The New Feminist Criticism.*
    see also: Hirsh, Marianne. *The Mother/Daughter Plot: Narrative, Psychoanalysis and Feminism* (Bloomington: University of Indian Press). 1989.
58. Goldstein, Rebecca. *The Late Summer Passion of a Woman of Mind.* (New York: Farrar, Straus and Giroux). 1984. 56.
59. *Time and Narrative.* I. 76.
60. Ibid. 57.

Chapter II

1. Ricoeur, Paul. *Oneself as Another.* trans. Kathleen Blamey. (University of Chicago Press: Chicago). 1992. 320.
2. Riocoeur, Paul. *Time and Narrative.* vol. I. trans. Kathleen McLaughlin and David Pellauer. (University of Chicago Press: Chicago). 1984. 39.
3. see, Mary Mason, "The Other Voice: Autobiographies of Women Writers," Doris Sommer, "Not Just a Personal Story: Women's *Testimonios* and the Plural Self," both in *Life Lines: Theorizing Women's Autobiography* ed. Bella Brodzki and Celeste Schenck. (New York: Cornell University Press). 1988.
   also see:
   Nancy Miller, *Feminist Alternatives* (Mississippi: University Press of Mississippi). 1990.
   Leigh Gilmore, *Autobiographics: A Feminist Theory of Women's Self-Representation* (New York: Cornell University Press). 1994.
   Elaine Showalter, *Women, Literature, and Theory.*
   Hirch Marianne, *The Mother/Daughter Plot: Narrative, Psychoanalysis, and Feminism.* (Bloomington: Indiana University Press). 1989.

4. see:
   Kant, Immanuel. "What is Enlightenment?" *Philosophical Writings*. trans. Lewis White Beck, ed. Ernst Behler. New York: Continuum. 1986.
   Adorno, Theodor, and Max Horkheimer. *Dialectic of Enlightenment*. trans. John Cummings. New York: Seabury Press. 1972.
   Vattimo, Gianni. *The End of Modernity*. Baltimore, Maryland: John's Hopkins University Press. 1988.
5. *The Spivak Reader* ed. Donna Landry and Gerald Maclean. (New York: Routledge). 1996. 101.
6. Ibid. 110.
7. *Reader*. 27.
8. "Acting Bits/Identity Talk." 774.
9. *Identity Talk*. 774.
10. It should be noted that even though this is a crucial aspect of Spivak's understanding of identity, she strongly cautions against using this idea of identity to further notions of group identity, political identity, or national identity.
11. *Reader*. 26.
    see also: Spivak, Gayatri. *In Other Worlds: Essays in Cultural Politics* (New York: Routledge). 1988.
12. Gayatri Chakravorty Spivak, "Acting Bits/Identity Talk" *Critical Theory*. 18. 4. Summer 1992. 770.
13. For a critique of Spivak's practice of citing her subject position and interests in the deconstructive process, see: Sangeeta Ray, "Shifting Subjects Shifting Ground: The Names and Spaces of the Post-Colonial" *Hypatia* 7. 2. Spring 1992. 188-189.
14. Butler, Judith. *Gender Trouble: Feminism and the Subversion of Identity*. (New York: Routledge). 1990.
15. Ibid. 16.
16. Ibid. 17.
17. Ibid. 4.
18. Ibid. 32.
19. Ibid. 31.
20. Ibid. 25.
21. Ibid. 142.
22. Ibid.
23. Ibid. 144.
24. Ibid.
25. Ibid. 17.
26. Ibid. 143.
27. Ibid. 145.
28. Ibid. 147.
29. *Women as Subjects: South Asian Histories*, ed. Nita Kumar (Charlottesville: University Press of Virginia). 1994.
30. Ibid. 4.
31. Ibid. 17.
32. Ibid. 20.
33. Ibid. 21.
34. Ibid. 11.
35. Ibid. 15.

36. Ibid. 25.
37. Ibid. 6.
38. Ibid. 310.
39. Ibid. 12.
40. Ibid. 6.
41. Ibid. 14.
42. Spivak, Gayatri, "Translator's preface" in Jacques Derrida's *Of Grammatology* (Baltimore: Johns Hopkins University Press). 1076. ix-xxxvii.
43. Ibid. 38.
44. see: *Feminist Postmodernism,* Linda Nichelson and Nancy Frazer.
45. Braidotti, Rosi. *Nomadic Subjects: Embodiment and Sexual Difference in Contemporary Feminist Critique.* New York: Columbia University Press. 1994. 35.
46. *Feminists Theorize the Political.* 7.
47. *Fault Lines.* 78.
48. Ibid. 80.
49. Ibid.
50. Ibid. 85.
51. Ibid. 107.
52. *Fault Lines.* Alexander, Meena. (City University of New York: The Feminist Press). 1993. 2.
53. Ibid. 3.
54. Ibid. 198.
55. *The Spivak Reader.* 27.
56. Ibid. 127.
57. *Fault Lines.* 25.
58. Ibid. 111.
59. Ibid. 119.
60. *Fault Lines.* 120.
61. Ibid. 125.
62. Ibid. 177.
63. Ibid. 182.
64. Ibid. 202.

Chapter III

1. Aristotle, *Poetics.* trans. Richard Janko (Indianapolis: Hackett Publishing Company). 1987. VII. 26-33.
2. Ricoeur, Paul. *Time and Narrative* vol. I, trans. Kathleen McLaughlin and David Pellauer. (Chicago: University of Chicago Press). 1984. 45.
3. Ibid. 33.
4. Ricoeur, Paul. *Time and Narrative* vol. II, trans. Kathleen McLaughlin and David Pellauer. (Chicago: University of Chicago). 1985. 8.
5. *Time and Narrative* vol. I, preface.
6. Ibid. x.
7. Ibid.
8. Ibid. 61.

9.   The other option is "carnivalistic" see 96-98.
10. *Time and Narrative* vol. I, preface.
11. *Fault Lines.* 5.
12. Alexander, Meena. *Fault Lines* (City University of New York: Feminist Press). 1993.
     16.
13. Ibid. 16-18.
14. Ibid. 19-20.
15. Ibid. 20.
16. Ibid. 21.
17. Ibid. 31.
18. Ibid. 26.
19. Ibid. 22-23.
20. Ibid. 177.
21. *Time and Narrative* vol. I. 39.
22. Ibid. 15.
23. Ibid. 18.
24. Ibid. 16.
25. Ibid. 65.
26. Ibid. 26-27.
27. Ibid. 69.
28. *Time and Narrative* vol. I. 70.
29. *Time and Narrative* vol. II. 20.
30. *Time and Narrative* vol. II. 70.
31. *Time and Narrative* vol. II. 28.
32. *Fault Lines.* 43.
33. *Time and Narrative* vol. II. 4.

Chapter IV

1.   see: Ricoeur, Paul. *The Rule of Metaphor: Multidisciplinary Studies of the Creation of
     Meaning in Language.* trans. Robert Czerny. (Canada: University of Toronto Press).
     1975.
2.   "More On Power/Knowledge" Gayatri Spivak, *The Spivak Reader* ed. Donna Landry
     and Gerald Maclean. (New York: Routledge). 1996. see 162-4.
3.   Ricoeur, Paul. *Oneself As Another.* trans. Kathleen Blamey. (Chicago: University of
     Chicago Press). 1992. 124.
4.   Ibid. 124.
5.   Johnson, Mark. *Moral Imagination: Implications of Cognitive Science for Ethics.*
     (Chicago: University of Chicago Press). 1993.
6.   Ricoeur, Paul. *Time and Narrative.* vol. II. 159.
7.   Ricoeur, Paul. *Time and Narrative.* vol. I. 35.
8.   see: *Diagnostic and Statistical Manual of Mental Disorders.* third ed. (American
     Psychiatric Association: Washington, D.C.). 1980. 253.
9.   Altering Ricoeur's category of "narrative" has implications beyond identity; it also
     effects the way one would make sense of time. Meena Alexander does not have a linear
     conception of time.

10. This is an extension of Spivak's understanding of *idam* and *aham,* and the substitution of the Sanskrit terms for the Latin ones addresses the narcissism that Spivak insists is the "touchstone of western imperial masculine identities." see: "Echo" in *The Spivak Reader* (New York: Routledge). 1996. 175-202.
11. *Autobiography: Essays Theoretical and Critical* ed. James Olney. New Jersey: Princeton University Press. 1980.
12. *Fault Lines.* 23.
13. Alexander, Meena. *The Poetic Self-Towards a Phenomenology of Romanticism.* (New Jersey: Humanities Press). 1979. 20.
14. Roland, Alan. *In Search of the Self in India and Japan: Toward a Cross-Cultural Psychology.* (New Jersey: Princeton University Press). 1988. 10.
15. Recall from the first chapters discussion of *The Rule of Metaphor* that the exciting aspect of metaphor, for Ricoeur, is its power to create new meanings through re-association. My alternative model of internarrative associations does not transcend the claims of *The Rule of Metaphor*, it liberalizes it while staying within the theoretical framework. Internarrative association, the creation of a plethora of new meaning, can be understood as a Ricoeurean project.

    Ricoeur's account of linguistic innovation rests upon the re-descriptive power of metaphor. Deconstruction, or what Ricoeur calls the hermeneutics of suspicion, does a useful thing; it reminds us of the arbitrary nature of the relationship between the signifier and the signified, but it stops there. Ricoeur thinks we should go further than Deconstruction toward what he terms a hermeneutics of faith. This is faith in the re-descriptive power of language. Rather than reducing reference, we should multiply reference. This is what I intend through internarrative associations.

Chapter V

1. Goldstein, Rebecca. *The Late-Summer Passion of a Woman of Mind.* (New York: Farrar, Straus and Giroux). 1989. 18.
2. Ibid. 134.
3. Ibid. 48.
4. Ibid. 172.
5. Ibid. 148.
6. Ibid. 260.
7. Ibid. 55.
8. Schafer, Roy. *Retelling a Life, Narration and Dialogue in Psychoanalysis.* (New York: Basic Books, Harper Collins). 1992. 23.
9. Ibid. 34.
10. Ibid. 30.
11. Ibid. 50.
12. Ricoeur, Paul. *Oneself as Another.* trans. Kathleen Blamey. (Chicago: University of Chicago Press). 1992. 124.
13. Ricoeur, Paul. *Time and Narrative* vol. III. trans. Kathleen Blamey and David Pellauer (Chicago: University of Chicago). 1985. 246.
14. *Retelling a Life.* 50.
15. Ibid. 52.

16. Ibid. 57.
17. Ibid. 56.
18. Ibid. 57.
19. Ibid. 57.
20. *Oneself as Another.* 147.
21. Ibid. 58.
22. Alexander, Meena. *The Poetic Self: Toward a Phenomenology of Romanticism* (New Jersey: Humanities Press: Atlantic Highlands). 1980. 20.
23. Blamey, Kathleen. "A Philosophical Itinerary from Ego to I to Self."

The translator of the three volumes of *Time and Narrative,* Kathleen Blamey, is interested in following and describing the complex route of the development of the notion of subjectivity in Ricoeur's work from "ego to I to self." There is no argument being made here. Hers is simply a "Philosophical Itinerary." But, again, her work is representative of recent Ricoeur scholarship. Let me explain.

She begins not with existential Phenomenology but with Ricoeur's mature "option for language." And she traces the development of the idea of a connection between language and subjective experience of time, to the conception of the self as a subject of action, as agent, as author, Blamey traces Ricoeur as he moves away from the vantage point of his Freudian investigations, and rather than viewing the ego in the position of master-consciousness, prefers to think of "I" as the subject of action. She describes hi interest in narrative against the backdrop of a prior interest in language, against a hermeneutical tradition. Ricoeur is not so interested in the hermeneutics of suspicion (the reductive hermeneutic described in the first chapter) but rather in a hermeneutics of trust which focuses on polysomy and the over determination of linguistic expressions. And Blamey accounts for the way in which Ricoeur's interest in language is bound up with the problem of time. But while Blamey underscores muthos as action she overlooks the very specific structure within which action can happen.

The author of the itinerary rightly points out that for Ricoeur narrative brings time to expression; it articulates an enigma of human experience. But when she makes a list of all the ways narrative can look (fairy tales, epics, drama, modern novel, chronicles and itineraries) she undervalues the structural form these narratives must take. What makes an itinerary narrative, for example, is its structure. There are three aporias that remain at the end of *Time and Narrative.* Listed in reverse, they are, first, the aporia of the "inscrutability of time." This refers both to that quality of time that remains inaccessible to conceptualization and the vestiges of the conception of time as something we find ourselves "in." The unrepresentability of time has led to fragmentary representations of time. The second aporia is one of totality and totalization which expresses the difficulty of reconciling the past, present, and future. This is the feeling that time is collective and singular. The third aporia is the split between phenomenological and cosmological time. This is the sense in which our lived experience of time is unable to account for physical time so that cosmological time (the time of physical nature and its units of measurement) cannot integrate subjective experience of time. Now, between these two types of time, Ricoeur attempts to create a third type of time, one which acts as a bridge between the time of the physical world and the time of our experiences. Things like clocks and calendars serve as a link because they mark cosmological time and human beings use them to place experience. Narrative identity involves the type of connection, this third sense of time.

Since Ricoeur's mature conception of self draws its intelligibility from a model of narrative theory, Blamey wants to delineate the narrative framework within which identity has meaning. But her account of the narrative framework in which identity-as-authorship is constituted, emphasizes Ricoeur's reliance on Aristotle's notion of *muchos* as action. She correctly notices that this sense of *muthos*, of structuring, is the "putting-into-the-form-of-a-plot (emplotment)" and mentions the imperative Aristotelian plot structure. Blamey is impressed by the way that, on Ricoeur's model, identity is revealed not in the description of events (and thus identity has little to do with the involuntary) but rather on creative re-description, *mimesis$_2$*. But the extent to which re-description is possible is limited to the assumed structure of the narrative. To liberalize structural requirements would be to enrich the notion of redescription.

As I have just stated the focus of Blamey's understanding of *muthos*, is on *muthos* as action and she undervalues the compositional requirement. *Muthos* is not the act of just any kind of emplotment; the action of *muthos* is limited by Aristotelian aesthetic requirements. The result is that Blamey understates the structural restrictions of self-formation. Blamey's account of Ricoeurean "self" focuses exclusively on the conception of self as the subject of action. She focuses singularly on social and political circumstances as the limit within which a self can act. But Ricoeur envisions the narrative self as emplotted not only in involuntary circumstances but also in narrative configuration. This itinerary does not record the detour of the ego through formal requirements in the process of self creation. In her description of the connection between subjectivity and time consciousness and narrative she hints at the structural requirement in saying that "forming a whole" is linked with a narrative model of comprehension. And the narrative function of bringing time to expression structures identity. The fact that the proto-typical narrative structure serves as model of intelligibility is represented as unproblematic. When she calls "configurational competence characteristic of narrative composition" by "configurational competence" she means several things (muthos as action, text as basic unit, etc.) but what she assumes but does not focus on is the whole/unified structure as the primary feature of Ricoeurean narrative. "Configurational competence" for Blamey means acting, practicing, emplotting, situating, contextualizing, narrating. In a more general sense, contextualizing ones life narratively. She does not focus on the ordering of discordant experience. Blamey sees identity as a "category of practice." What she does not focus on, what she barely even mentions, is the structural requirement. I am not arguing that Blamey misreads Ricoeur or makes any kind of crude mistake. I am pointing out that even though Blamey assumes the structural requirement of Ricoeurean narrative, she focuses on the functions of narrative over its features and therefore focuses on narrative as an act and identity as a process. She overlook the manner in which assumed structure of narrative structures identity.

24. Dauenhauer, Bernard. "Ricoeur and Political Identity" *Philosophy Today.* Spring, 1995. 47-55.

Bernard Dauenhauer has come up with the interesting project of extending Ricoeur's conception of personal identity to the political realm—to political identity. Dauenhauer's pragmatic inclination is to distrust most claims to political identity. He wonders about a basis for discriminating between defensible and indefensible political identities, and finds in Ricoeur's account of personal identity conditions which are applicable to a defendable political identity. In fact, he insists that the only appropriate kind of political identity would be an extension of Ricoeurean person identity. But he makes two mistakes. First, while he is interested in narratives which constitute political identity, he does not take into account the aesthetic criteria for narrative and therefore overlooks determining structure. He mistakenly argues that "... the narratives relevant to the constitution of personal identity are always partial." This oversight, along with the second mistake, the mis-reading of *ipse,* lead him to the conclusion that a Ricoeurean political identity would be based on a "partial" narrative which allows for a change in commitments. Dauenhauer thinks that narratives of political identity which satisfy this requirement encourage societies members not to give unqualified allegiance to any concrete state of their political society, "My Ricoeurean proposal . . . provides considerable insurance against adopting or countancing political identities that are tyrannical." This conclusion is questionable at best. But I would like to address the second problem first.

Dauenhauer finds a troubling part of political identity, as commonly understood, its over-reliance on its unique characteristics (*idem*) and its devaluing of *ipse.* He is not included toward political identity defined by the groups distinguishing characteristics (*idem*) and thinks that the only kind of defensible political identity is one which is developed through common commitment. But I don't think Dauenhauer's reading of *ipse* captures its essence or all its implications. One with *ipse*-identity would honor a political commitment even if ones values have changed. For Ricoeur, keeping one's promise even if one's values, convictions, and projects have changed, "does indeed appear to stand as a challenge to time, a denial of change: *even if my desire were to change*" (emphasis is mine). This means that, "even if I were to change my opinion or inclination, I will hold firm." "*Ipse*" involves keeping a promise *in spite of changes in convictions.* This is precisely the opposite of the way Dauenhauer understands *ipse.* Actually the aspect of political identity which he is critical of (lack of interest in the reform of commitments) would be supported by Ricoeur's understanding of *ipse.*

Secondly, Dauenhauer overlooks the aesthetic requirements for narrative structure. He insists that the "narratives relevant to the constitution of personal identity are always partial." Then Dauenhauer lists the ways in which he thinks Ricoeurean narratives are open-ended. First, he says, Ricoeurean narratives exclude some experience that they could include. Second, these narratives make "contestable distributions of emphasis" among the items they do include. And third, there are always alternative versions which could be told and these alternative versions could have a different emphasis and could be inclusive of other types of experience. The argument is that Ricoeurean narratives are partial in these three ways and this is important because the stories this type of theory can yield are in inexhaustible supply. But these elements of partiality are effects of the discordance of experience that Ricoeurean emplotment attempts to suppress. I am not arguing that these three elements of partiality, defined as they are, are not present in Ricoeurean narrative, but they are present *in spite of emplotment.* The three aspects of partiality listed above seem to me to actually be three objections to Ricoeurean narrative rather than three features of it. For example: the first element (that narrative excludes some experience it could include) is precisely the element that makes narrative *whole,* according to Ricoeur. This is the desired result of concordance.

Ultimately in order for political identity to be defensible on Dauenhauer's account, its narratives must have several features: 1, They must be partial. 2, The narratives must admit that every political society impinges upon other societies. 3, A defensible narrative must admit that its society might become obsolete. 4, The narrative must not claim to possess the definitive word about its own defensibility. The job of political narrative is to help a society top recognize these features of its situation. Only the first of these four requirements is Ricoeurean. Ricoeur does not concern himself too much with the content of narratives and the second through fourth narrative requirements are requirements about content. And Dauenhauer does not claim that these requirements are Ricoeurean, just that the "partial" structure, and the emphasis on changing commitment, are taken from Ricoeur. But I do not think that even these two requirements can be attributed to Ricoeurean narrative theory or personal identity theory. By "partial" Dauenhauer means structurally (his first feature) and content-wise. I object only to the first sense. Recall from previous chapters how adamantly Ricoeur insists upon unified and whole structure. According to Ricoeur, a partial structure would be excluded from the realm of narrative altogether. Though the last stage of *mimesis, mimesis₃*, takes place in the reader, the internal structure of the work itself must be closed. That is to say that a narrative should be internally closed (have an ending) while retaining an open-ended involvement with the reader's world. This is *mimesis₃*. Any narrative which does not conform to the formal features of Aristotelian muthos, the criteria of unity and completeness, represents for Ricoeur, the end of the paradigmatic tradition of emplotment. And the end of this tradition is something that he laments. Ricoeur is interested in the "deep structure" which manifests in concrete narrative configuration on the surface of the narrative. The structural analysis of perennial narrative paradigms is motivated by the "ambition to ground the narrative function on structural rules" and to impose a "logical type of rationality" on the production of narrative. This reduction is characterized by three features. First, it is a deductive procedure. This means that because there are such a variety of narrative expressions, there should be a hypothetical "model." Secondly, it should be modeled upon linguistics in the sense that the code should be separated from the message. And systematic organization should be "mastered" by the act of structuring, which is defined as "a closed set of internal relations between a finite number of units." Third, there should be priority of the whole over the parts. This Ricoeur says, is the most important of the three features.

On my reading of Ricoeurean personal identity, the extension of personal identity to political identity, would involve a process wherein political identity is created in the narrative process of the mediation between permanent defining characteristics of the group, and the commitment of the group to remain faithful to its commitments in spite of changing values. These elements are precisely when Dauenhauer does not want in his notion of political identity.

25. Joy, Morny. "Writing as Repossession" forthcoming in *Narrative Texts and Contrasting Contexts: The Impact of the Work of Paul Ricoeur.* (Canada: University of Calgary Press).

26. Kristeva, Julia. *In the Beginning There Was Love: Psychoanalysis and Faith.* trans. A. Golhammer. (New York: Columbia University Press). 1887. 8.

27. Benstock, Shari. "Authorizing the Autobiographical" *The Private Self: Theory and Practice of Women's Autobiographical Writings.* (Chapel Hill: University of North Carolina Press). 1988.

28. Joy. "Repossession." 4.

29. see: *Time and Narrative* II. 20-32. and *Oneself as Another* 143, 148-57.

30. Joy. "Repossession." 4.

31. see: Ricoeur, Paul. *Freedom and Nature: the Voluntary and the Involuntary.* trans. Erazim V. Kohak. (Illinois: Northwestern University Press). 1966.

32. Danica, Elly. *Don't: A Woman's Word.* (Dublin Ireland: Attick Press). 1988.
33. Allen, Charlotte Vale. *Daddy's Girl.* (New York: Wyndam Books). 1980.
34. Frazer, Sylvia. *My Father's House.*
35. Aristotle. *Poetics* vii. 27-30.
36. Joy. "Repossession." 9.
37. Frazer. 250.
38. Joy. "Repossession." 9.
39. Joy. "Repossession." 11.
40. Joy, Morny. "Feminism and the Self" *Theory and Psychology.* vol. 3(3): 275-302. (Canada: Sage Publications).
41. Joy. "Feminism and the Self." 396.
42. Joy. "Feminism and the Self." 280.
43. Ibid. 295.
44. Ibid. 299.
45. see also: Joy, Morny. "Reflections of Ricoeur's *Oneself as Another*" *Three Loves: Philosophy, Theology, and World Religions.* (Georgia: Scholars Press). 1994.

Bibliography

Alexander, Meena. *The Poetic Imagination: Toward a Phenomenology of Romanticism.* New Jersey: Humanities Press. 1980.

————. "Exiled By a Dead Script" in *Contemporary Indian English Verse: An Evaluation,* ed. Chirantain Kulshrestha. New Jersey: Humanities Press. 1981.

————. *Women in Romanticism.* Maryland: Barnes and Noble Books. 1989.

————. *Fault Lines.* City of University of New York: The Feminist Press. 1993.

————. (Interview with Meena Alexander by Susie Tharu) in *Journal of South Asian Literature* vol. 2 n1 winter/spring. 1986. 11-23.

Allen, Charlotte Vale. *Daddy's Girl.* (New York: Wyndham Books). 1980.

Armstrong, Nancy. *Desire and Domestic Fiction.* Oxford: Oxford University Press. 1987.

Armstrong, Paul. *The Challenge of Bewilderment: Understanding Representation in James, Conrad and Ford.* Ithaca: Cornell University Press. 1987.

————. Conflicting Readings: Variety and Validity in Interpretation. Chapel Hill: University of North Carolina Press. 1990.

Bakhtin, Mikhail. *The Dialogic Imagination,* ed. Michael Holquist, trans. Caryl Emerson and Michael Holquist. Austin: University of Texas Press. 1981.

Bateson, Mary Catherine. *Composing a Life.* New York: Plume. 1990.

Benstock, Shari. "Authorizing the Autobiographical," *The Private Self: Theory and Practice of Women's Autobiographical Writings.* Chapel Hill: University of North Carolina Press. 1988.

Booth, Wayne. *The Company We Keep: An Ethics of Fiction.* Berkeley: University of California Press. 1988.

Braidotti, Rosi. *Nomadic Subjects: Embodiment and Sexual Difference in Contemporary Feminist Theory.* New York, Columbia University Press. 1994.

Bruner, Jerome. *Actual Minds, Possible Worlds.* Cambridge, Mass: Harvard University Press. 1986.

Chatman, Seymour Benjamin. *Story and Discourse: Narrative Structure in Fiction and Film.* Ithaca, New York: Cornell University Press. 1978.

Clark, S. H. *Paul Ricoeur.* New York: Routledge. 1990.

Culler, Jonathan. *Structuralist Poetics: Structuralism, Linguistics, and the Study of Literature.* Ithaca, New York: Cornell University Press. 1975.

Danica, Elly. *Don't: A Woman's Word.* (Dublin Ireland: Attic Press). 1988.

Dave, Shilpa. "The Doors to Home and History: Post Colonial Identities in Meena Alexander and Bharati Mukherjee" in *Amerasia Journal.* vol. 19 n 3. 1993. 103-113.

Goldstein, Rebecca. *The Late Summer Passion of a Woman of Mind,* New York: Farrar, Straus and Giroux. 1989.

Heilbrun, Carolyn. *Writing a Woman's Life.* New York: Ballantine. 1988.

————. Reinventing Womanhood. New York: Norton. 1979.

Iser, Wolfgang. *The Act of Reading: A Theory of Aesthetic Response.* Baltimore: Johns Hopkins University Press. 1978.

————. *Prospecting: From Reader Response to Literary Anthropology.* Baltimore: Johns Hopkins University Press. 1989.

————. *The Fictive and the Imaginary.* Baltimore: Johns Hopkins University Press. 1993.

Johnson, Mark. *Moral Imagination: Implications of Cognitive Science for Ethics.* Chicago: University of Chicago Press. 1993.

Joy, Morny. "Derrida and Ricoeur: A Case of Mistaken Identity (and Difference)" in *The Journal of Religion,* vol. 68 n 4. October 1988.

————. "Feminism and the Self" in *Theory and Psychology.* Canada: Sage Publications. 1993.

————. "Writing as Repossession: The Narratives of Incest Victims" in (upcoming) *Narrative Texts and Contrasting Contexts: The Impact of the Work of Paul Ricoeur.* Canada: University of Calgary Press.

————. "Reflections of Ricoeur's *Soi-meme comme un autre*" in *The Three Loves: Philosophy, Theology, and World Religions.* Atlanta, GA: Scholars Press. 1994.

Kristeva, Julia. *In the Beginning There Was Love: Psychoanalysis and Faith,* trans. A Golhammer. (New York: Columbia University Press). 1987. 8.

Life/Lines: Theorizing Women's Autobiography, ed. Bella Brodzki and Celeste Schenck. New Jersey: Cornell University Press. 1988.

Lloyd, Genevieve. *Being in Time: Selves and Narrators in Philosophy and Literature.* Routledge: New York. 1993.

MacIntyre, Alasdair. *After Virtue: A Study in Moral Theory.* Indiana: University of Notre Dame Press. 1981.

Miller, J. Hillis. *Ariadne's Thread: Story Lines.* New Haven: Yale University Press. 1992.

Narrative in Culture: The Uses of Storytelling in the Sciences, Philosophy, and Literature, ed. Cristopher Nash. New York: Routledge. 1990.

Olney, James. *Metaphors of Self.* New Jersey: Princeton University Press. 1972.

Philosophy of Paul Ricoeur, ed. Lewis Hahn. Carbondale: Southern Illinois University. 1995.

Ricoeur, Paul. *Fallible Man,* trans. Charles A. Kelbley. New York Fordham University Press. 1986.

————. *Freedom and Nature: The Voluntary and the Involuntary,* trans. Erazim V. Kohak. Northwestern University Press. 1966.

————. *Freud and Philosophy: An Essay on Interpretation,* trans. Denis Savage. New Haven: Yale University Press. 1970.

————. *The Rule of Metaphor: Multi-Disciplinary Studies of the Creation of Meaning in Language,* trans. Robert Czerny. Canada: University of Toronto Press. 1977.

————. *Time and Narrative,* vol. I, trans. Kathleen McLaughlin and David Pellauer. Chicago: University of Chicago Press. 1983.

————. *Time and Narrative,* vol. II, trans. Kathleen McLaughlin and David Pellauer. Chicago: University of Chicago Press. 1985.

————. *Time and Narrative,* vol. III, trans. Kathleen McLaughlin and David Pellauer. Chicago: University of Chicago Press. 1988.

————. "Narrative Identity" in *Philosophy Today.* Spring 1991. 73-80.

————. *Oneself as Another,* trans. Kathleen Blamy. Chicago: University of Chicago Press. 1992.

————. *Freud and Philosophy: An Essay on Interpretation,* trans. David Savage. New Haven: Yale University Press. 1970.

Roland, Alan. *In Search of Self in India and Japan: Toward a Cross-Cultural Psychology.* New Jersey: Princeton University Press. 1988.

Schaffer, Roy. *Retelling a Life: Narration and Dialogue in Psychoanalysis.* New York: Harper Collins. 1992.

Shotter, J. *Conversational realities: Constructing life through language.* Thousand Oaks, CA: Sage. 1994.

Tompkins, Jane. *Sensational Designs.* Oxford: Oxford University Press. 1985.

Walker, Nancy. *Feminist Alternatives: Irony and Fantasy in the Contemporary Novel by Women.* Mississippi: University Press of Mississippi. 1990.

White, Hayden. *Metahistory: Six Critiques.* Middletown, Conn: Wesleyan University Press. 1980.

Winslade, J. and L. Hedtke. Michael White: Fragments of an Event. *The International Journal for Narrative Therapy and Community Work, 2008* (2), 2008. 73-79.

Women as Subjects: South Asian Histories, ed. Nita Kumar. Charlottesville: University Press of Virginia. 1994.

Index

About the Author

Ajit Maan holds a B.S. in Journalism, a M.S. in English Literature, and a Ph.D. in Philosophy. Her areas of specialization include philosophy in literature and classical and postmodern aesthetic theory. Maan lives with her family in Oregon, where she is currently at work on a collection of philosophical essays.